BIBLE-BEL~~~~~~~~~~~~~

SHOULDN'T ~~~~~~~~~~~DDING

or

The Bible

what is it?
how did we get it?
how shall we use it?

Stephen B Dawes

(c) Stephen B Dawes, 1993
ISBN 0 9520644 0 5
Southleigh Publications   4 Upland Crescent
Truro   Cornwall   TR1 1LU

All rights reserved. No part of this book may be reproduced or transmitted in any form or by any means including recording or photocopying, without permission in writing from the publisher.

British Library Cataloguing-in-Publication Data. A catalogue record for this book is available from the British Library.

Printed by Mid Cornwall Printing, Truro
from the author's origination

Easter 1993

Dear Reader

Thank you for buying this book. Despite its silly title it is not a silly book.

You have in your hands a small but a serious book about the Bible and the Methodist Church. It is, I hope, a careful study of the place of the Bible in the Methodist Church. This is a controversial issue at the moment, as some Methodists feel that our Church today no longer believes in the Bible or takes much notice of what it says. So I want to look at how the Bible is used in the Methodist Church today, and what authority it has for us in the 1990's. But before we can look at that question it is necessary to look closely at the Bible itself, at what it is and what it isn't, and at how it came to us. For any belief about the place which the Bible ought to have in the Church, or about its inspiration and authority must begin from the Bible itself, and must take the Bible as it is very seriously. I hope that taking the Bible seriously is what I do throughout this little book.

If by any chance you are not a Methodist but have got this far, I hope you won't stop reading now. I am a Methodist, writing for Methodists and using Methodist illustrations, but the issue of the place and authority of the Bible is one that every denomination of the Christian Church is having to face up to today. I guarantee that my illustrations will not be very far from what is happening in your Church too, and the wider questions apply to us all.

Rev Dr Stephen B Dawes

Chairman of the Cornwall District
of the Methodist Church

Most of the Bible quotations in the book are from the New Revised Standard Version of the Bible, copyright 1989 by the Division of Christian Education of the National Council of the Churches of Christ in the U.S.A. All quotations from Methodist statements, reports or other publications are acknowledged where they are found, and are used with permission.

CONTENTS

1. "This is the Word of the Lord" — 4
2. "Madam President" — 9
3. "The Bible says...." — 14
4. The Methodist Church says.... — 19
5. Living up to expectations — 23
6. But not just like any other book either — 28
7. Back a stage - how we got our Bibles — 36
8. Two sorts of details — 45
9. So what can we say about the authority and inspiration of the Bible? — 53
10. Divorce, Black Pudding and other things — 58
11. Like a mobile — 65
12. The Human Sexuality Report — 70
13. But what about slippery slopes? — 80
14. Taking the Bible seriously in other matters too — 82
15. But what about the nasty bits? — 90
16. The last word? — 93
17. Some books and things about the Bible — 96

<u>1</u>   "This is the Word of the Lord."

The Christian Faith, no matter which church or denomination we belong to, believes that the Bible is uniquely special and important. For Christians the Bible is the "Holy Bible." It is the "Word of God." For all the churches there is no other book, or collection of books, like it. The Bible is inspired, and it speaks with authority.

I cannot think of anywhere where this is put more clearly than in the first verse of the old hymn by Bishop William Walsham How [1823-97],

>*"O Word of God incarnate,*
>   *O wisdom from on high,*
> *O truth unchanged, unchanging,*
>   *O light of our dark sky,*
> *We praise thee for the radiance*
>   *That from the hallowed page,*
> *A lantern to our footsteps,*
>   *Shines on from age to age."*

[<u>Hymns and Psalms</u> 478]

The hymn says that the Bible is God's wisdom and truth, a shining light to guide us. The first verse seems to say that the Bible is the "Word of God incarnate," unique among books, and verse three goes on to call it the "chart and compass" of the Christian Faith.

No matter which denomination of the Christian Church we belong to, the special place of the Bible in the Christian Faith will be seen very clearly in what goes on in worship on a Sunday. In almost every service of worship there will be two or even three readings from the Bible, and many churches use a Lectionary to make sure that they cover as much as possible of the Bible every two or three years. In what used to be called the Free Churches, such as the United Reformed Church, the

Baptists or the Methodists, there will be a sermon which will often be seen as the climax of the whole service, and that sermon will almost certainly be based on a verse or passage from the Bible. Among recent developments in Roman Catholic worship there has been the insistence that at every Mass there should be a comment on the Bible reading. Worship in the House Churches or the Pentecostal Churches will be free and informal, but here too the Bible takes centre stage in teaching as well as in worship. In many Anglican services you will no longer hear the old "Here ends the lesson" at the end of each Bible reading; instead you are more likely to hear the reader say,

"This is the word of the Lord,"

to which the congregation will reply,

"Thanks be to God."

Listening to the Bible, and then hearing its stories or teaching explained seems to be an important part of Christian worship. Why? Because the Bible is "the Word of the Lord."

The special place of the Bible in worship can also be seen in church architecture and design, and in some of the customs associated with reading the Bible in services. Many of our Methodist chapels in Cornwall are built around large central pulpits from which the Bible is read and the sermon on it is preached. Many of our Parish Churches have ornate lecterns from which the Bible is to be read. Most places of worship have beautiful and expensive Bibles for the lectern or the pulpit, even if some of these have now seen better days. In some churches worship begins when a Bible is carried in and placed at the front while the congregation stands. It is the custom in Anglican and Roman Catholic churches for the congregation to stand while the Gospel reading is read, and this reading is often preceded by a procession with candles and the kissing of the Holy Book. Some churches provide Bibles in the pews, and members of the congregation are encouraged to follow the readings for themselves. In all of these ways the Bible is seen and used in the churches as an important part of worship. It is indeed seen as a special book. It is the "Holy Bible." In it we expect to hear the "Word of the Lord."

It is also a remarkable fact that the Bible continues to be a "best-seller," which means that people in large numbers must be buying it. No doubt they buy it for all kinds of reasons, but it looks as if it is important to many people, outside of the churches as well as inside, to have their own personal copy of the Bible. Christians of every denomination are encouraged by their churches to read the Bible for themselves as part of their personal devotions and prayers, and as part of their Christian discipleship. So it is that Members of the Methodist Church are reminded on the annual Membership Ticket that they should be committed to "prayer and Bible Study." And it is for this reason that a Bible may be presented when someone is received into Church Membership or confirmed, or when a young person leaves their local church to go to college or university. Reading the Bible is widely seen as essential for a Christian, a vital part of our personal discipleship.

Because reading the Bible is something that many Christians believe they ought to do and want to do, there are nowadays many organisations and publications which offer help and guidance for those who want to read their Bibles. There are, for example, a whole variety of Bible Reading Notes and Guides pitched at all levels from child to adult and from beginner to expert now easily available. In addition many churches put on Bible Study sessions. All of this is done because the Bible is felt to be important in the life of the church and for the spiritual health or growth of the Christian. Similarly because reading and understanding the Bible is important, a flood of new translations have appeared. Since the *New English Bible* started the trend in the 1960's there have been, according to my calculations, no less than six important new translations of the Bible into modern English. So in addition to its special place in the worship of the churches the Bible is obviously believed to be an important book for all Christians to have, to read and to use.

So far the churches seem to agree with the Bishop and his hymn that the Bible is uniquely special and important, that it is God's shining light to guide us. But then we come up against the fact that in many of the churches the Bible is strangely silent. Many churches do not have Bible Study groups, and those which do often find them poorly attended. I have no way of knowing how many church members buy and use Bible Reading Notes of any kind, but I suspect that it is only a small minority. The Bible readings in church services are themselves so bitty that they are often hard to follow or grasp. The result is that many Christians are amazingly ignorant of what the Bible says, as are most people in our contemporary society. I was listening recently to *Brain of Britain*, or one of the programmes like it, and none of the contestants could answer a question about how many loaves and fishes there were! This is serious. For one thing it allows people to be hoodwinked by those who confidently assert that "The Bible says," and groups like the Mormons and the Jehovah Witnesses are cashing in on this ignorance. Preachers and teachers have to be on their toes too, for gone are the days when Bible stories or illustrations could be used in sermons with a simple, "You remember the story of ...," because many in our congregations today don't, although they sometimes feel guilty that they ought to.

At the same time the Bible is the source of considerable controversy in the church today. I shall give some examples in later chapters, but all I need to say here is that it is sometimes said that the real divisions in the church today are not those between the different denominations. Today's divisions, it is said, are between "conservative" and "radical," "fundamentalist" and "liberal," or "traditionalist" and "modernist," and these divisions cut across the denominational boundaries. At the heart of these new divisions and at the core of many of our controversies today lie differences in understanding the Bible. No one disagrees with general statements about the importance of the Bible. Of course it is a *"lamp to our feet and a light to our path"* as it says in Psalm 119:105, and of course Christians have to take its teachings seriously: but problems begin when different groups find different points of view in the Bible, and each group then claims to be doing or believing what the Bible says. Or there is trouble when some Christians come to conclusions about what we should believe or what we should do on the basis of general principles which they find in the Bible, while others come to different conclusions on the basis of actual texts of Scripture. Then again there are those who believe that decisions about right and wrong should be made only on the basis of what the Bible says, while others think that other things need to be taken into account as well. Christians might agree on the importance of the Bible, but they don't agree on how the Bible is to be understood, applied or used.

Do the churches agree with the Bishop's hymn that the Bible is uniquely special and important? Do they believe that it is God's shining light to guide us? The answer is "Yes and No." Yes, the churches do say that the Bible is special and important: but No, it doesn't seem to be God's clear shining light to guide us. We inherit the Bible as a book which we use within the church, a book that speaks with authority, a book that we treat with respect, but which we also neglect at times. We use it for all kinds of things. In preaching and in teaching it has pride of place. We use it to justify and defend beliefs which we hold, and more questionably, as a weapon for attacking those who hold different opinions. Instead of being something that holds the church together, the Bible is a potent source of conflict and disagreement among Christians.

It looks as if it is a very easy thing to say that the Bible is the "Word of the Lord." But it is much harder to agree on what it is saying to us. In the next chapter I will give a simple illustration of the problem.

2 "Madam President."

Something special happened at the Methodist Conference held in Newcastle upon Tyne last June. There on Saturday June 27th the Methodist Church in the United Kingdom appointed its first-ever woman President of the Methodist Conference. Shortly after 3pm the Rev Kathleen M Richardson was duly elected by a Standing Vote as President of the Conference, and then inducted into office. She had been the first woman minister to become a District Chairman [we still call her a "Chairman" because we haven't thought of anything better yet] when she became the Chairman of the West Yorkshire District in 1987, and now she is our first woman President of Conference. For the first time in our history those who spoke in the Conference had to begin by saying, "Madam President," instead of the "Mr President" which probably goes right back to the days of the first Conferences under the Reverend Mr Wesley himself.

We in Cornwall were priviledged to have the President visit the Cornwall District as her first District visit after taking office. I personally felt thrilled to be the first District Chairman to be welcomed into office by a Woman President when Kathleen conducted my welcome service at Camborne Wesley on August 29th. Wherever we went around the District that weekend I was conscious that the Methodists of Cornwall were delighted to have Kathleen and her husband amongst us.

So in the Methodist Church 1992 must go down as a good year for women. It was the year in which we recognised and celebrated the gifts of women as we appointed our first woman President of the Conference.

There is no doubt at all that Methodism in Cornwall or anywhere else could not exist today without women in the ministry, women Local Preachers and the leadership of women in all kinds of offices in our circuits and local churches. We don't keep statistics on this one but I think the figures are that about a quarter of our two thousand or so Methodist ministers in the active work are women. By contrast the figures for the Cornwall District are that we only have 4 women ministers out of a total of 57. Methodism has had women Local Preachers for donkey's years, and at a rough count about a third of the active Local Preachers in this District are women. Without them many of our pulpits would be empty, and Superintendent ministers would not be able to make their Plans. I have no statistics for the numbers of women on our Church Councils or Circuit Meetings, but my experience in the old Bodmin circuit was that the men were heavily outnumbered. Last but not least there is the position of the Vice-President of the Conference, the highest honour that Methodism has to offer a lay person. Since Methodist Union in 1932 there have been twelve women elected as Vice-President, including our own Pamela Luke in 1982. The Methodist Church relies heavily on the commitment and leadership of women at national, Circuit and local church levels, in every part of our organisation and in the leading of our worship.

1992 was also a good year for women in the Church of England, at least in my opinion, when on Wednesday November 11th the General Synod made its historic decision to admit women to the priesthood. Whether that decision was a good one for the Church of England is, of course, another question; and answers to that one differ widely and sadly. There are many people in the Diocese of Truro who have been deeply hurt by the Synod's decision. I listened to the Synod debate on the television and the arguments were fascinating. One point that came up was that it would be wrong to admit women to the priesthood because the Bible plainly prohibited it. Does not the Bible say that women should not have authority over men? Therefore women should not be priests!

The same sort of arguments were heard when Methodism was discussing whether or not we should have women ministers, which was decided on at the Manchester Conference in 1970. We had had women preachers for years, as well as Wesley Deaconesses who in many cases did everything that ministers did anyway: but the arguments were still heard, "The Bible says that women should not be ministers."

In fact the Bible says something much stronger than that. The Bible says that women should not even speak in church, and that women should not have authority over men. The text I have in mind and which was quoted in some of our Methodist discussions in 1970 was this:

> *"As in all the churches of the saints, women should be silent in the churches. For they are not permitted to speak, but should be subordinate, as the law also says. If there is anything they desire to know, let them ask their husbands at home. For it is shameful for a woman to speak in church."*
>
> [I Corinthians 14:34-35]

Here St Paul is giving an explicit rule about the place of women in the church. On this score instead of appointing a woman President and encouraging women to hold office in church we ought to stop women preaching and ask all women office-holders to resign their posts immediately.

So here we face a serious question. The Bible forbids women to speak in church, yet in the Methodist Church we encourage women to become Local Preachers and Ministers of the Gospel. If the Bible forbids women to speak in church how does the Methodist Church dare to permit them and encourage them? And the Methodist Church is not alone in this, the other Free Churches have had women ministers for a lot longer than we have, and the Church of England has women Deacons who preach as well as women Readers who conduct worship. How can all this be?

The answer that is usually given to this question goes like this. When St Paul wrote these words forbidding women to speak in church he meant exactly what he said, but his command was for a particular church [the church in Corinth] at a particular time [about thirty years after the death of Jesus] and for a particular reason [Corinth was a funny place, and already had more than its fair share of odd religions.

In some of these women led all sorts of goings-on of which St Paul, and you and I, wouldn't approve. St Paul did not want the Christian church in Corinth to be confused with those sorts of religious sects. Therefore he ruled that Christian women should be silent in church]. This line of argument accepts that there were good reasons for St Paul to say there and then what he did say. Then it goes on to say that we need to recognise that circumstances alter cases. We live in a different place, at a different time, and in very different circumstances: therefore we are not bound by the precise command of this text.

You might disagree with that line of argument, and you are quite at liberty to do so. And you will find that there are Christians who forbid women to speak in their churches because they believe that what St Paul said applies to us today precisely as he said it. In their churches the women will probably also* wear hats because St Paul insisted on that too, see 1 Corinthians 11 verses 5 and 10. Those churches which don't insist on women wearing hats, interpret St Paul's command about that in just the same way as his command about women keeping silent. My question to those Christians who do not allow women to speak in church, or who insist on women wearing hats in church is "Do you eat Black Pudding?" But that comes later.

The argument about whether or not the Bible allows women preachers and ministers is actually more complicated than this one verse from 1 Corinthians. Those who say that 1 Corinthians 14:34-35 is not the last word on the subject usually point to another text from one of St Paul's writings,

> "There is no longer Jew or Greek, there is no longer slave or free, there is no longer male or female; for all of you are one in Christ Jesus."
>
> [Galatians 3:28]

On the basis of this they say that here St Paul has grasped the principle of the equality of the sexes, and that as far as the life and work of the church is concerned the distinctions between male and female are as irrelevant as those between Jew and Greek or slave and free. The church is a new creation in which these distinctions have no place. You then have to try to weigh up the "general principle" of Galatians 3:28 against the specific ruling of 1 Corinthians 14:34-35. Again, you are free to disagree with the conclusion that the general principle should be given more weight than the specific ruling.

Just to finish off the argument about women preachers and women in positions of leadership in the church, the last stage in saying that the ruling in 1 Corinthians 14:34-35 is not the last word is usually the one of showing that in the New Testament itself there were women preachers and leaders. From another of St Paul's writings we can include in this number Phoebe the deacon, Prisca and her supportive husband, and the woman apostle Junia [Romans 16:1,3 and 7].

The Methodist Church, along with other churches, allows women to preach, to hold office and to have authority and exercise leadership. We also allow women to come to church without a hat! We do these things despite clear Bible texts that say that women should not do any of them. The Bible says one thing, and says it clearly: but the Methodist Church does quite the opposite. And I don't think that there are many Methodists who bat an eyelid about it on this question of women preachers and women ministers. Some Methodists might moan about some women preachers, and some circuits might still be reluctant to have women ministers: but not because the Bible says so.

If I speak at the Methodist Conference to be held in Derby next June I will have to begin my speech with the words, "Madam President." For the President of the Conference is Rev Kathleen Richardson, who is a woman Methodist Minister and the one who has final authority over me in the life of the Methodist Church. But should this be so? We call the Bible the "Word of the Lord" but at the same time we seem to feel free not to listen when it speaks. What then about the authority and the inspiration of the Bible? That is the important question that this book is all about. To begin to answer it we will first look at what claims the Bible makes for itself? So that's where we go next.

3   "The Bible says...."

In this chapter we begin to look at that pair of crucial questions that every reader of the Bible comes to sooner or later, and usually sooner. These are the controversial but central questions about the *authority* of the Bible and the *inspiration* of the Bible. In the first chapter we saw the important place given to the Bible in all the churches, but then in the last chapter we saw that on the question of women preachers the Methodist Church and other churches as well choose to ignore what the Bible explicitly teaches.

So in this chapter I want to look at what authority the Bible itself claims to have. Those Christians who believe that the Bible has a unique authority in the Christian Faith usually justify their belief by reference to the special inspiration which they believe the Bible has. The Bible speaks with authority, they believe, because it is the inspired "Word of God." Some of those who believe this believe that every word of the Bible was directly inspired by God, whilst others believe that it was the Bible writers who were inspired by God in a unique way. Either way, the Bible speaks with authority because it is inspired by God.

One text in particular is quoted by those who believe that the Bible has a special authority because of its divine inspiration. This text is 2 Timothy 3:16-17, and it is the only place in the Bible where the word "inspiration" is used about the Bible,

> *"All scripture is inspired by God and is useful for teaching, for reproof, for correction, and for training in righteousness, so that everyone who belongs to God may be proficient, equipped for every good work."*

There is actually a slight problem with this text straight away, because there are two ways of translating the first line which gives two rather different meanings. The NRSV gives the other possible translation in a footnote,

> *"Every scripture inspired by God is also..."*

I propose to leave that little problem on one side even though the second way of translating the line changes the meaning of the verse a lot. In what follows I shall use the first version, which is the one quoted by those who use it to support their views on the special authority and inspiration of the Bible. The translation in the new NRSV is much the same as that of the old *Authorised Version*, which was,

> *"All scripture is given by inspiration of God, and is..."*

I need to comment on only three of the words or phrases in this text:

a) *"All scripture..."*

The word "scripture" means "holy writing / "holy book" or "holy writings / "holy books". In the previous verses the writer has advised Timothy to continue to be faithful to the truth he has known for a long time, and to the *"sacred writings"* which he has known since childhood [verse 15]. He then goes on to say that each of these holy books, inspired by God, and all of them together, are useful in equipping Timothy and every other Christian for God's work and service.

Timothy would have been in no doubt about what books were meant. The "scriptures" he had known since childhood were the books of what we call the "Old Testament." At the time that this letter was written the scriptures of the first Christians would have been the books of the Old Testament, not quite in the same order as in our Bibles and certainly including what today we call the "Apocrypha." The books which we know as the "New Testament" were only then in the process of being written, and were not accepted as scripture in the form in which we have them now until several hundred years after the life of Christ, as we will see in chapter 6.

b)   "...*inspired by God*..."

   This phrase translates a single word found only here in the whole of the Bible. The *New International Version* translates it literally, "God-breathed." The scriptures which Timothy has known from childhood are "God-breathed." They are "inspired." A small problem with this is that because this word is only used here in the whole of the Bible we cannot be absolutely certain what it means, but its general sense is plain enough. These scriptures come, one way or another from God. It is his life which flows through them. It is his breath that gives them voice. So far so good.

   It can also be argued on the basis of this word that the scriptures have a special and powerful authority because they are "God-breathed" in a way that no other book or collection of books is "God-breathed." Some Christians might disagree and say that this goes beyond what the text actually says, but most Christians would be happy to say that one way or another the Bible is one of God's special gifts to us. So far so good also.

   But at this point those who use this verse to back up their belief in the inspiration of the Bible usually take a giant leap forward, and go way beyond what this word means or this text says. This leap is to argue that because the scriptures are "God-breathed" they must therefore be without error. They are inspired, therefore they are infallible. So a doctrine of the infallibility or the inerrancy of scripture is established without any argument, and with only the simple assumption that if God is breathing into these books they must be without error.

   That is a huge leap into a dangerous doctrine. It is a leap without any evidence or support from the word "God-breathed" or from the verse where this word is found. Those who want to say that because the Bible is God-breathed it is without error are making an assumption. Neither more nor less than an assumption. What they ought to do next is to show from the Bible itself that it is a valid assumption and a true doctrine, but this simply cannot be done. In chapter 5 I shall show from the Bible itself that there are errors within its pages. And one error is enough to show that

16

the assumption that because the Bible is inspired it is without error is a false one.

c) "... useful..."

What a let-down! Timothy is reminded that the scriptures which he has known since childhood are "useful"! This adjective is found in only two more places in the New Testament. In Titus 3:8 it is translated "profitable" and in 1 Timothy 4:8 it is translated "of some value." If the word "God-breathed" means what some people say it means, then the words of God in the scriptures ought to be a jolly sight more than useful. They would surely be much more than "profitable?" They would be the answer to everything. They would be the key to the meaning of life, the universe and everything. Instead Timothy is reminded that they are "useful," "helpful."

Moslems believe that the Quran is God-dictated, that it was actually dictated word for word to Mohammed by the angel Gabriel in God's presence. They then go on to draw the logical conclusion from their belief. If these words are inspired in this way then they are to be revered and reverenced. They are to be memorised word for word, hallowed and obeyed. They are the final answer to everything. Any Moslem who said that the Quran was only "useful" would soon be in trouble with his local Imam. But that is all that this verse says about the holy books that Timothy has known since childhood, that they are "useful." No more. No less. The scriptures which God has given are a helpful thing to have for teaching about God, his will and his ways.

So what claims does the Bible make for itself? From the Bible itself what do we learn about its authority and its inspiration? Let me repeat myself. 2 Timothy 3:16 is the key text used by those who believe that the Bible has a special authority because of its divine inspiration, and this verse is the only place in the Bible where the word "inspiration" is used about the Bible. The verse does talk about the importance and the value of the scriptures, and I for one would not want to deny either of those things, but all that it says is that scripture is "useful." This famous text says nothing about the historical accuracy or reliability of the Bible. It makes no claims that the Bible is "without error." It does not claim that the Bible is the supreme authority in the Christian Faith. It is not even talking about any of the Bibles we actually use, for none of them existed in the forms we have them when these words were written. 2 Timothy 3:16 is the key text about the authority and inspiration of the Bible, yet the claim it makes is only a very modest one. Next we must look at what claims the Methodist Church makes about the Bible. What does Methodism believe about the authority and inspiration of the Bible?

4   The Methodist Church says ...

What does the Methodist Church say about the Bible? What does it believe about the Bible's authority and inspiration?

The easiest place to start is with Question 52 in the <u>Methodist Catechism</u> which was approved at the Stoke on Trent Conference in 1986,

> 52. What is the Bible?
>
> *The Bible, comprising the Old and New Testaments, is the collection of books, gradually compiled, in which it is recorded how God has acted among, and spoken to and through, his people. The writers expressed themselves according to their own language, culture and point in history and in their different ways were all bearing witness to their faith in God. The Bible is the record of God's self-revelation, supremely in Jesus Christ, and is a means through which he still reveals himself, by the Holy Spirit.*

Notice the six points in the answer:

1   The Bible is not one book but a collection of books, gathered together over a long period of time,

2   The Bible contains the record of how God acted among his people and spoke to them,

3   The writers were real people who expressed themselves in the language and forms of their day,

4   The writers in the Bible saw things differently and wrote in different ways, but each one is expressing his faith in God,

5   The Bible shows us how God was making himself known to us,

6   The Bible is one of the ways in which he still makes himself known to us.

The "Title Deed" of the Methodist Church is the <u>Deed of Union</u> of 1932, agreed upon by the three branches of Methodism which came together again in that year to form the Methodist Church as it now is. The Doctrine of the Methodist Church is dealt with in Section 2 of the Deed, in a section of only eleven short paragraphs taking up a page and a half of the <u>Deed of Union</u>'s thirty pages. The Bible is dealt with in the second full paragraph in Section 2:4, where it states that,

> *"The doctrines of the evangelical faith which Methodism has held from the beginning and still holds are based upon the divine revelation recorded in the Holy Scriptures. The Methodist Church acknowledges this revelation as the supreme rule of faith and practice ..."*

I gather that this wording came from the great Primitive Methodist layman and Biblical scholar, Professor A S Peake, whose "<u>Peake's Commentary on the Bible</u>" has helped many a student over the years.

This is a very carefully worded statement, and we should notice what it says and what it doesn't say:

1   It says that our Methodist doctrines *"are based upon the divine revelation recorded in the Holy Scriptures"* and that Methodists acknowledge *"this revelation as the supreme rule of faith and practice."* It does not say that the Bible is our supreme rule of faith and practice.

2   It says that *God's revelation recorded in the Bible* is our supreme rule of faith and practice. It does not define what it means by *"God's revelation recorded in the Bible"* - is this revelation the words of the Bible themselves, or is it what the words are talking about, the great events of the Old Testament and the stories of Jesus?

3   It does not say that "*the Bible* is the supreme authority for the Christian." It says that *God's revelation, which is recorded in the Bible*, is the supreme authority for the Christian.

4   It does not say that our Methodist doctrines are taken straight from the Bible. It says that our doctrines are *based on* God's revelation which is recorded in the Bible.

5   And it doesn't even say what it means by *the* Holy Scriptures! Does it mean the Old and New Testaments, like the Catechism says, or does it include any of the books of the Apocrypha?

As far as I know these are the only two official statements which the Methodist Church makes about the Bible.

I want to end this short chapter, however, with reference to an "unofficial" Methodist statement about the Bible. In the new Local Preachers' Training Course, called "Faith and Worship," unit 5 is about the Bible and is called, "*Exploring the Bible.*" This unit looks at what the Bible is, how it came to us, which books belong to it, and at the variety of different kinds of writings found within its pages. Then in section 7 it comes to the question we are looking at in this book, "*The authority of the Bible.*" The unit does not give any answers but it asks the Local Preachers on Trial who are doing the course to think about various aspects of the question. One of the tasks it sets them is to look at this diagram,

| The Bible is the dictated word of God, containing no errors, and everything in it is literally true. | The Bible is the fallible product of human beings and must be given no more authority than any other book written. |

[--]

and then to ask themselves : What are the errors with both of these positions?

The question which the students are asked assumes that both of these positions are wrong. I think that whoever it was who thought up that diagram and decided on that question has understood the Methodist statements on the Bible which we find in the <u>Deed of Union</u> and in the <u>Catechism</u>. These official statements suggest that both of the positions expressed in the diagram are wrong, and that a true position on the question of the authority of the Bible is going to lie somewhere on that line between the two extreme positions which are quoted.

In the next chapter I want to look at what is wrong with the first position, at why we cannot put the Bible on a pedestal as high as that. In the one after I shall look at what is wrong with the second position, at why we cannot treat the Bible just like any other book.

5   Living up to expectations.

What is wrong with saying that

> "The Bible is the dictated word of God, containing no errors, and everything in it is literally true?"

There are some Christians who have no trouble at all with what this statement says about the Bible, and there are some Methodists among them. I have heard people say this sort of thing in discussions about the Bible in many different places. But on what grounds do they say it and believe it? Often they say that they believe it because the Bible itself says so. But we have already seen in chapter 3 that the main verse that is quoted to support this statement actually says nothing of the sort. Those who think this about the Bible cannot argue that the Bible says this, for it doesn't. In the end their argument is a statement of personal opinion, and like all statements of personal opinion, mine included, it needs to be tested. In this case we need to test the statement against the Bible itself, to see if its claims are justified.

In the rest of this chapter I will concentrate my fire on the second phrase in the statement, that the Bible *contains no errors*. I will show that the Bible does contain some simple and straightforward errors. I concentrate on this phrase because it is the easiest of the three statements to test - all we have to do is read what the Bible actually says. If we read the Bible and find that it can be seen to contain errors then the other two parts of the statement fall apart. For if the Bible had been *dictated* by *God* it wouldn't contain any mistakes: if we find mistakes this must show that God could not have *dictated* it. And if we find mistakes in the Bible, then obviously *everything in* the Bible can't be *literally true*.

What do I mean by an "error?" For the sake of

simplicity I shall look at only one sort of error, the simple contradiction between Bible passages which are talking about the same thing.

If my car is photographed going through red traffic lights by those new cameras we don't have in Truro yet, and I say that my wife was driving and she says that I was, then there is an error in our two statements. Her statement might be right, or mine. Or it might not have been our car at all, or the camera might have been faulty, or it might have been our daughter driving. None of these things affect the fact that there is a contradiction between our statements, which shows that there is an error somewhere in the whole business. The court will try to get to the facts of the case: but the simple contradiction between our statements has brought the police to our door because they see from this contradiction that there is something wrong somewhere. In the following examples of contradictions in the Bible I shall not make any attempt at all to get to the bottom of the case, to say who or what is right, or what might have really happened. That is the job of the court. I am just the policeman who has noticed that two statements contradict each other, and who says that there is something wrong somewhere!

Here then is a little list of straightforward errors, some big, some little. Just one would be enough to prove that it is not true to say that the Bible *contains no errors*, but here are a dozen for good measure:

1 Who actually discovered that the tomb was empty on that first Easter Day?

    Was it Mary Magdalene and *"the other Mary"* as Matthew 28:1 says?
    Or was it Mary Magdalene, Mary the mother of James, and Salome as Mark 16:1 says?
    Or was it Mary Magdalene, Joanna, Mary the mother of James, and other unnamed women as Luke 24:10 says?
    Or was it Mary Magdalene and Simon Peter as John 21:1-2 says?

2   Did Abraham know and use God's personal name?

Exodus 6:3 says No;
Genesis 12:7, 13:4 and 15:7 say Yes.

3   Did Mary and Joseph take Jesus to Egypt after his birth or not?

Matthew 2:14 says Yes; Luke 2:39 says No.

4   How many of each species of "clean" animals went into Noah's Ark?

Genesis 6:19 says one pair; Genesis 7:2 says seven pairs.

5   When did Jesus cleanse the Temple?

On an early visit to Jerusalem as in John 2:13-22?
Or on the Sunday before he was crucified as in Matthew 21:12-17?
Or on the Monday before he was crucified as in Mark 11:12-19?

6   What was the real reason for observing the Sabbath Day?

Was it that *"in six days the LORD made heaven and earth, the sea and all that is in them, but rested the seventh day; therefore the LORD blessed the sabbath day and consecrated it,"* as in Exodus 20:11?

Or was it *"that you were a slave in the land of Egypt, and the LORD your God brought you out from there with a mighty hand and an outstretched arm; therefore the LORD your God commanded you to keep the Sabbath day,"* as in Deuteronomy 5:15?

7   Who were the Twelve Disciples?

There is no problem with eleven of them in the lists of disciples found in Matthew 10:2-4, Mark 3:16-19, Luke 6:14-16 and Acts 1:13. But who was the twelfth man? Was it *Thaddaeus* as in Matthew and Mark, or was it *Judas son of James* as in Luke's lists in his gospel and Acts? Or was it even *Lebbaeus* whose name is found in some ancient manuscripts of Matthew's gospel, or was Lebbaeus another of Thaddaeus's names as other old manuscripts have it?

8   How much did King David pay for the land on which he hoped to build the Temple?

Was it the bargain price of fifty shekels of silver, as in 2 Samuel 24:24, for which he got some oxen thrown in as well? Or was it six hundred shekels of gold, as in 1 Chronicles 21:25?

9   What was the last thing Jesus said from the cross?

Did he cry, *"It is finished,"* as in John 19:30?
Or did he cry, *"Father, into your hands I commend my spirit"* as in Luke 23:46?

10   Who was Jesus's paternal grandad?

Jacob as in Matthew 1:16 or *Heli as in* Luke 3:23?

11   Did one of the dying thieves believe in Jesus in the end?

Yes, according to Luke 23:39-43: but No according to Matthew 27:44 and Mark 15:32.

12   Did God create a man before he created the animals, or after?

After according to Genesis 1:24-27.
Before according to Genesis 2:18-20.

Let me repeat myself again. In this chapter I am not asking whether or not God created the world, or how he did it. I am not asking if Jesus really was raised from the dead or what really happened at the first Easter. I am not asking if these Bible passages are true to life, or true to science or true to history. That is for the court to decide. I am just asking if the statements tally. And they don't, as you can see by looking at the statements I have quoted.

Some of these twelve examples are about very important issues, others are about quite trivial ones.

But all of them are simple and straightforward examples of statements in the Bible which contradict other statements. If the one answer is right, the other must be wrong. There is an error somewhere. On this score alone the position that says that,

> *"The Bible is the dictated word of God, containing no errors, and everything in it is literally true"*

is simply untenable. There are contradictions in the Bible, the most easy to demonstrate and basic of all errors. If that part of the argument of this position cannot hold, and it clearly can't, the rest falls with it.

6   But not just like any other book either.

What is wrong with saying that

> "The Bible is the fallible product of human beings and must be given no more authority than any other book written?"

After all, we have just seen in the last chapter that the Bible is indeed fallible. And we saw in chapter 3 that the Bible is really quite modest in the authority it claims for itself. So it looks as if there might not be very much wrong with this statement. But appearances are deceptive.

I started the last chapter by saying that I had often heard Christians make the sort of statement that we were discussing in that chapter. But I have never heard anyone make the statement we are looking at now. I know many Christians who say that the Bible is fallible. I say so myself. I know many Christians who say that sometimes we give the Bible too much authority. I say that as well. But I have never heard a Christian make the statement that we are discussing here.

So what is wrong with it? For a start the Methodist Church doesn't believe it. And for another thing none of the other churches believe it either. We saw in chapter 1 how all the churches value the Bible as a special book; they all treat it quite differently from any other book. We saw in chapter 4 that the Methodist Church also treats the Bible as a special book, or collection of books, saying that in the Bible we have the record of how God has shown himself to us; the Bible is precious because it records God's revelation. It is a simple matter of fact that Christians venerate the Bible in a way they do no other book or books. Most denominations have special books which they value for different reasons, and we Methodists have always set great store by our hymn books and, officially at least, by Wesley's Sermons: but great though we value these, we would not dare to put them in the same class as the Bible. All the churches insist that when it comes to the question of the Bible's authority, then the Bible is not like any other book written.

To fill this answer out a little bit I need to use a technical term, and I think I've not done badly to get this far without using any technical terms at all. The technical term I need to use now is *"canon."* For reasons that are now impossible to state, first the Jews and then the Christians decided that they needed a "Bible," a collection of sacred writings, and virtually every Christian denomination and Jewish group since then has accepted those collections. Not only does the church give the Bible more authority than any other book written, as we have seen, but it also gives the books of the Bible more authority than any other books written. And actually the good books came before the Good Book.

The fact is that the church has put a fence around certain books. Inside the fence are a small number of special books, while left outside are hundreds of other Christian writings of all kinds. Or to put it another way, the church has made a list. It has made a list of special books which it considers to be the sacred scriptures of the Christian Faith. The books on this list, and only those books, are to be regarded as the "official documents" of Christianity. This official list is the "canon of sacred scripture," the list of books which the church considers to be special. We know this "canon of sacred scripture" as the "Bible." Rightly or wrongly the church decided that it needed a list of official books, and once that list was compiled the books on it were treated as special books whether they deserved it or not. So the books of our Bibles have been collected together and stamped as "official" by the church, and that gives them a special authority.

Of course there have been all sorts of other books which Christians have read with profit over the centuries, and many other books which have been valued and appreciated by the churches. But they never made the official list. The official list is a short one and it has been closed for over fifteen hundred years. Just by being on the list books like Daniel, the Gospel of John and the First Letter to Timothy have an authority and a status that other books no matter how old, or beautiful or spiritual do not have.

You might disagree with all of this and say that the church should not have a "canon" at all, that it is wrong to have an "official list" of "approved books." Or you might want to question the church's wisdom in including some of the books they included in their list and leaving out some of those they chose to leave out. Or you might think that we should have an open list, a sort of loose-leaf Bible, so that we can add some new books occasionally and weed out some of the old ones. I have heard all those things suggested in one place or another. But the fact is that the "canon" exists. The churches have a list of sacred writings which by its very existence sets the books on the list apart from all others. The books on that list do have, as a matter of fact and as a result of the church setting up that list, more authority for Christians than any other books written.

Unfortunately at this point there is a complication. For there is not one agreed "official list" but several. There are a number of different "canons of sacred scripture." There are different Bibles read in different churches - not different translations, there are plenty of those - but different *Bibles*.

The Bible which you will find in most Methodist pulpits is likely to be either a *Good News Bible*, my favourite version for use in worship, or an *Authorised Version*, the old translation of 1611 with its beautiful but totally out of date English which rightly belongs in a museum and not in a church in the 1990's. Both of these versions have 39 books in their Old Testament part, starting with *Genesis* and ending with *Malachi*, and 27 books in their New Testament part, going from *Matthew* to *Revelation*. But if you were to look in your local Roman Catholic church you would see that the Bible in the pulpit there is a bit different. It will probably be a *New Jerusalem Bible*, and it will have 7 extra books in its Old Testament part, as well as extra chapters in the books of *Esther* and *Daniel*. Its New Testament will be the same as ours and it will still go from *Genesis* to *Revelation*. Most modern translations nowadays, like the *Revised English Bible*, are available with these extra books separated out under the heading of the "Apocrypha," or the "Deutero-canonical books." But the newest and best modern translation for study use, the *New Revised Standard Version*, has even more books in its Apocrypha. In addition to the extra books from the Roman Catholic Bible it has books from the Bibles of the Greek and Slavonic Orthodox Churches as well.

In all of these different Bibles the New Testament is the same. In all of them you will also find the 39 books of the Old Testament which we are familiar with: but in the Roman Catholic and Orthodox Bibles you will find different extras. The reason for this is that the Old Testament of the "Protestant Bible," as ours is sometimes called, only has those books which are found in the Hebrew Bible, and which are read and used in synagogues today. The other Bibles add extra books which were used by Greek-speaking Jews outside of Palestine but which did not get onto the approved list of sacred scriptures agreed upon by the Jewish Rabbis. Just like us, the Jews drew up an official list, and the 39 books of our Old Testament are that list – though just to complicate matters still further, we put them in a different order!

Thus we have in all Christian Bibles 39 Old Testament books and 27 New Testament books, with a dozen or so extra books floating around which some churches regard as just as weighty and official as the 66 but others don't. Traditionally the Protestant churches have chosen to disregard the extras, while the Roman Catholics have approved their own extras and disregarded the Orthodox extras, and vice versa. In fact this used to be a highly controversial subject, but generally speaking I don't think the churches get too worked up about it any more. The Methodist Church statements I quoted in chapter 4 can be safely assumed to be talking about the Old Testament of 39 books, and there is no official statement that I know of about the extras. But the important point about all of this is that it was the churches which drew up their lists of sacred books. It was the churches which decided what the Contents Page of the Bible they would use looked like! It was the churches which decided which books went on the list and which ones did not.

All sorts of fascinating questions spring to mind next: how did they decide? How did they choose which books to put on their official list of sacred scripture and which to leave off? How did they make their minds up? When and where did they make these decisions? Who had the final say?

Sadly there are not too many detailed answers: but the detectives have pieced the puzzle together like this:

1   The Old Testament of 39 books.

The Hebrew Bible is divided into 3 parts. The first and most important is the "Law" [often called by its Hebrew name, the *Torah*], and this consists of the five books from *Genesis* to *Deuteronomy*. Second comes the "Prophets," which consists of *Joshua, Judges, Samuel* and *Kings* in one group and *Isaiah, Jeremiah, Ezekiel* and the twelve shorter prophets in another. The last part is the "Writings," which consists of the rest.

Scholars believe that the first two parts were recognised as sacred scripture by the Jews by about two hundred years before the time of Jesus, the opening verses of the prologue to the *Book of Ecclesiasticus* giving them one of the most important clues. The New Testament also refers to the "Law" and the "Prophets" as if they were recognised sacred writings whose teaching had to be taken seriously. When the "Writings" were given the status of sacred scripture is not quite so clear. It used to be said that this was at the Council of Jamnia, a kind of Rabbi's Conference around 100 AD, but that is only guesswork, and there is a possibility that it was a couple of hundred years before that.

We can't be sure of many of the details of the process: we don't know why these 39 books were chosen, nor do we know anything much about who made the decisions, when or where. We do know that some of the Rabbis kept on arguing about some of the decisions for many years, for their arguments are found in the Talmud, the ancient great encyclopaedia of the Jewish Faith. They argued over such questions as, should *Ecclesiastes* be in or not? There was even discussion about *Ezekiel*. And we shouldn't be surprised that some uptight Rabbis thought that the *Song of Songs* definitely shouldn't be there. It is clear from the Talmud too that the order of the books took some time to settle down. But eventually the list was settled. The Jewish Faith had a list of official scriptures. The Hebrew Bible with its 39 books had arrived. Full stop.

2   The Old Testament extras.

At the time of Jesus more Jews lived outside Palestine than inside it, and most of them spoke Greek. So the books they read and used in their worship and schools were translated from Hebrew into Greek. At the same time all sorts of other books were written in Greek by Jews and valued by the large Jewish communities in such places as Egypt. When the Christians came on the scene they preferred reading the Greek translations of the ancient scrolls rather than struggling with the original Hebrew, for Greek was the everyday language of the Mediterranean world. But the Rabbis in Jerusalem didn't like Greek, and they were in charge. Their list of sacred scripture had no Greek books in it. It was the Hebrew Bible, take it or leave it, and the early Christians left it. They carried on using the scriptures in Greek, the 39 books plus the "extras."

When Latin replaced Greek as the language of the Western World it was this bigger Greek Old Testament which was translated into Latin. So when St Jerome [round about 390 AD] set out to produce a new Latin Bible which was to be translated from the Hebrew and not the Greek he had a problem, what did he do with the Greek extras? He wanted to call them "extras" because he agreed with the Rabbis, but in the end they appeared in his Old Testament, and have done in Roman Catholic Bibles ever since. Meanwhile in the Eastern Church where they carried on speaking Greek they naturally carried on using the bigger Greek Bible with even a few more extras added.

The reason why we Protestants use the 39 is simple. At the Reformation in the sixteenth century the great reformers, Luther and Calvin, wanted to "get back to the Bible," and decided that the only Bible to get back to was the Hebrew one. No doubt the fact that their great enemy, the Church of Rome, used the longer Greek version played some part in their decision. They were the ones who called these extra books, "apocrypha," a rather rude term which originally referred to books by heretics which were best hidden: but the title has become respectable since then.

3   The New Testament

One thing is clear and that is that the early Christians did quite a lot of writing. St Paul wrote more letters than we have in the New Testament [see Colossians 4:16], and we know about a number of general books [eg the *Didache* (= the "Teaching"), the *Shepherd of Hermas*] as well as about other gospels [eg the *Gospel of Thomas*], other "Acts" [eg the *Acts of St Peter*], other letters [eg the *Epistle of Barnabas*] and other books like Revelation [eg the *Apocalypse of Peter*]. Why were our 27 chosen and these others rejected?

The detectives say that the process of selection worked on various principles, an important one being that for a book to be given the official stamp of approval it had to have been written by an apostle. Another factor was that the book in question had to be seen to be theologically correct: but that was a bit of a problem because you had no clear definitions to measure the book against. Whatever the reasons a list of special books gradually emerged, even though some of the books in our final 27 were disputed, *Hebrews* and *Revelation* in particular. We know about various lists from the end of the second century AD which are getting quite near to the list of our 27 books, and the great Christian scholar Origen [who died in 254 AD] had two lists, one of "acknowledged" books and one of "disputed" books. Among his disputed books he listed *James, Jude, 2 Peter, 2 and 3 John* and *Hebrews*. The first time that our 27 books are listed without any question or comment, though not quite in the order we are used to, is in the Easter Letter written by Athanasius, Bishop of Alexandria in Egypt, in 367 AD, but even then some disputes continued in the Western Church.

So it was all a long and gradual process. Local churches had their own sets of books which they prized and used, but we cannot talk about THE New Testament until around 400 AD. Of course the Christians through those centuries had the Old Testament and a large number of Christian writings which they used and valued, but they did not have an agreed and approved official list. They did not have a Bible in the way we have a Bible.

We cannot answer half of those fascinating questions about how my *Good News Bible* comes to have the 66 books on its Contents Page which it does have, or how my *New Jerusalem Bible* comes to have a few more. But what we can say is that the church or the churches, in one way or another, created the Bibles that we have. Whoever dictated, wrote or edited the individual books, it was the church which wrote the Contents Page. It was the church which decided that these 66 books, or 66 plus those extras, were to go on the list.

So what is wrong with saying that

"The Bible is the fallible product of human beings and must be given no more authority than any other book written?"

There might be several answers to the question: but a simple one is that the churches give the Bible more authority than any other book written, in the same way that they give the books they chose to go in the Bible more authority than any other books written. The full reasons why the church decided to follow the example of the Jews and set up a list of special books are now impossible to know, as it is also impossible to know why the Jews decided they needed a Bible after managing without one for centuries. The fact is that they did, with the result that we have a list of sacred writings, a Bible, and that 66 books or more are on it and in it. Now just being on the list gives these books an authority that other books do not have, because the churches give the Bible a special authority. Originally those books got on the list in the first place because believers saw in them something valuable, special and precious.

Perhaps a fuller answer lies in what I want to look at in the next chapter. Here we have looked at how 66 or more books get onto the official list, in the next chapter we shall be looking at how they came to be written, read and valued in the first place.

7   Back a stage - how we got our Bibles.

In the last chapter we looked at how the churches selected 66 books or so out of all the others that were around to make up their collections of official documents that we call the Bible. We saw how they borrowed the Old Testament ones from the Jews, then juggled them into a different order. We saw how the New Testament collection gradually came together over many years. With this background you can see why the Methodist Catechism describes the Bible as a *"collection of books, gradually compiled."* For modern Christians who, as we saw in chapter 1, take it for granted that the Bible is central to the life and work of the church, it can come as a bit of a shock to learn that our Christian ancestors did not have a Bible in the way that we do for over three hundred years! For most of that time they had holy books which they valued and took very seriously, turning to them for guidance on all sorts of questions about belief and behaviour, but no Official Book or Official Collection.

In this chapter I want to look at how the books which were chosen by the churches to go on the official lists got to that stage in the first place. In chapter 5 I hinted very strongly that it was nonsense to say that the books were "dictated by God," for if he had dictated the words there would not have been the errors I pointed out in that chapter, unless you then said that the "secretaries" he used were plain incompetent. The dictation idea is not a good one though for a better reason, because it does not have much support from the pages of the Bible itself. Here I want to look, as briefly as I can, at what clues the different books of the Bible give us about how they came to be written. The Bible I am using for this is the standard "Protestant" one, that is the 66 book version, and the particular translation is the recently published *New Revised Standard Version.*

The Hebrew Bible calls the first five books of what

we call the "Old Testament," the books from Genesis to Deuteronomy, the "Torah" or the "Law," as we have seen already. These books tell of the creation of the world, God's call of Abraham and what happened to his descendents at the time of Moses. This ancient title for these books was used by Jesus, who also called them the "Books of Moses" and who believed like all the Jews of his day that Moses wrote them [see for example Mark 12:26]. This was an old idea, but the five books themselves make no such claim. They are anonymous. No writer's name appears at the beginning or the end. They include many of Moses' speeches, and Moses is certainly the central character but nowhere in those five books is Moses said to have written them all. At Deuteronomy 31:9 Moses is said to have written down the "law" which he had been telling them about in the previous 26 chapters [Deuteronomy chapters 5-31], and Exodus 24:4 says that he wrote down the rules God had given him on Mt Sinai: but that is all that is said. Scholars disagree about how much of these five books goes back to Moses himself, and how they reached the form that we have them in today is also a matter of debate. It looks as if all sorts of old stories, rules, lists and songs, some of which had been written down for years, others of which had been passed down by word of mouth, were eventually collected, edited and published as God's *Torah*, his Revelation, Guidance and Law: but why, who by, when and where remains something of a mystery.

After Deuteronomy come a variety of "history books," from Joshua to 2 Kings. They tell the story of the people of Israel from the entry into the Promised Land under Joshua to their expulsion from it by the Babylonians about 6 centuries later. Then comes a repeat of it all in 1 and 2 Chronicles. All of these books are completely anonymous. Occasionally they mention older books that have been referred to by the writers or editors, and they may well contain some actual old historical records, but here too there is no simple answer to the questions of who wrote the originals and who put the collections together.

Next come two books whose authors seem to be named which tell of what happened in Jerusalem when the Jews returned from exile in Babylon. First is the Book of Ezra, part of which is written in the first person by

Ezra himself [eg 8:29], and then the Book of Nehemiah, his "Words" as it says at the very beginning.

Then we have two more anonymous books named after their chief characters, Esther and Job, before arriving at the Book of Psalms which is a hymnbook. Just like in our hymnbook some of the hymns are anonymous while others have the name of the author or the arranger or the collector at the top. It is generally agreed these days that the Book of Psalms as we have it was the hymnbook of the Temple that was rebuilt in Jerusalem after the return from exile in Babylon and consecrated in 516 BC, though many of the psalms go back to the first Temple that King Solomon built.

The Book of Proverbs is a collection of collections of proverbs or wise sayings attributed to King Solomon, as it says at the beginning. A second collection begins in chapter 10, and another in chapter 25. At 22:17 the heading *"the words of the wise"* introduces thirty sayings which were borrowed from an Egyptian writer. Tagged onto the end are the *"words of Agur"* [chapter 30] and *"the words of King Lemuel"* which his mother had taught him [chapter 31]: but who these men were no one knows. Likewise no one knows when these collections were put together or who by.

The Book of Ecclesiastes has a title, *"The words of the Teacher, the son of David, king in Jerusalem"* and here are two unsolved problems at once: first what the word translated "Teacher" really means, and second, who is meant. If it is referring to King Solomon his third book in a row comes next, for Ecclesiastes is followed by the book of love poetry called the Song of Solomon [or the Song of Songs].

From Isaiah to Malachi at the end of the Old Testament we have books which give us the teaching of the powerful preachers we call the "prophets" or which tell us stories about them. Each of these books is named after the prophet whose words they record or whose story they tell. There is great variety in what the books contain and in how the prophets came to speak, but the opening verses of most of the books are similar and set the scene for what follows. For example the Book of Isaiah begins *"The vision of Isaiah son of Amoz, which* he saw...," and chapter 2 is headed, *"The word that Isaiah son of Amoz saw..."* His vision in chapter 6 is well known. Other prophets too had visions which they then described to those who would listen, as the opening verses of the books of Ezekiel, Obadiah and Nahum show. But the prophets also spoke as if they were repeating what God had told them. So the Book of Hosea begins,

"The word of the LORD that came to Hosea...."

as do the books of the prophets Jeremiah, Joel, Jonah, Micah, Zephaniah and Malachi. Some use the technical term "oracle" to say the same thing, as in the opening of the books of Nahum, Habakkuk and Malachi. Thus in the books of the prophets we find such expressions as *"Thus says the LORD,"* and the prophets speak in the name of God, as in the famous verse from the Book of Jeremiah which we quote in the Covenant Service,

"The days are surely coming, says the LORD, when I will make a new covenant with the house of Israel and the house of Judah." [Jeremiah 31:31]

Here though it is Jeremiah who is speaking, the message is God's, and the prophet is his mouthpiece. The next chapter of Jeremiah shows this clearly. It begins,

"The word that came to Jeremiah from the LORD..."

and in it Jeremiah explains to the King who has imprisoned him for speaking out that he has spoken out because that is what the LORD had instructed him to do, and that what he had been saying was not his own opinion but what God wanted to be said. The prophets were thought to be in close touch with God, though that did not prevent King Jehoiakim burning the scroll on which Jeremiah's secretary had written down his master's message from God [Jeremiah 36]! We see from this incident that Jeremiah had a secretary who wrote down his words, and Isaiah gives us a clue about how his visions and sermons were preserved, for in Isaiah 8:16 he talks about "binding up the testimony" and "sealing the teaching" among his disciples. It looks as if the books of the prophets are collections of the sayings of the prophets, some long and some short, produced and edited later on by persons unknown. The belief was that the prophets were God's messengers, and the books with their names in the title were the record of his messages. This is very neatly put in the opening verse of the Letter to the Hebrews in the New Testament,

> "Long ago God spoke to our ancestors in many and various ways by the prophets."

At the end of this dash through the Old Testament we should note that apart from the speeches of these prophets who quote what God has said, the only other part of the Old Testament which claims to be dictated by God is the bit where Moses wrote down what God had told him on the top of Mt Sinai. The other thing to note, though I have obviously not been able to go into any detail at all, is that each and every book in the Old Testament has evolved or grown into its present form. Some of the books that we have were put together using parts of older books, others used old stories and sayings which had never been written down before. One of the things that some Old Testament scholars enjoy is the detective work in following up the clues and unravelling the strands in this process.

The New Testament begins with four gospels which tell the "good news of Jesus Christ, the Son of God" [Mark 1:1], and two of them tell us why they were written. The Gospel of Luke begins with these words,

> "Since many have undertaken to set down an orderly account of the events that have been fulfilled among us, just as they were handed on to us by those who from the very beginning were eye-witnesses and servants of the word, I too decided, after investigating everything carefully from the very first, to write an orderly account for you, most excellent Theophilus, so that you may know the truth concerning the things about which you have been instructed."   [Luke 1:1-4]

Notice what Luke says - that he has "investigated everything carefully" so that he can tell Theophilus, whoever he was, in an "orderly" way about those things that Theophilus has been taught. He knows that "many" others have already tried to do this, and now he has decided to have a go as well.

Nearly at the end of the Fourth Gospel we find this explanation of why that gospel was written,

> "Now Jesus did many other signs in the presence of his disciples, which are not written in this book. But these are written so that you may come to believe that Jesus is the Messiah, the Son of God, and that through believing you may have life in his name."   [John 20:30-31]

Here John admits to selecting and organising his material with one end in view, to get the reader to come to believe in Jesus in the same way that John himself does. He has written so that the reader might come to faith in Christ.

Perhaps this explains the many differences between the Fourth Gospel and the other three, for anyone reading John's gospel and any one of the others can't help but be struck by the differences. In the first three gospels Jesus spends all of his ministry in or around Galilee before journeying up to Jerusalem for the last week of his life: but in the Fourth Gospel Jesus goes to and fro to Jerusalem all the time. The teaching style is very different as well. In the Fourth Gospel we have long and involved arguments and gone are the short and often sharp parables which feature so much in the other three.

In contrast to John, anyone who reads the first three gospels can't help but be struck by the similarities between them. Many of the same miracles and the same parables occur in each one, well you'd expect that wouldn't you, and our very difficulty with the Fourth Gospel was that we didn't find what we might have expected. But then when we look at the tiny details we often find that two of these gospels agree but the third is different. Starting from this observation [check it out for yourself by comparing Matthew 19:13-15, Mark 10:13-16 and Luke 18:15-17] New Testament scholars have concluded that Mark was the earliest of the three to be written, and Matthew and Luke copied from his gospel. At the same time there was also a collection of the sayings of Jesus in existence which they also used. Each of them then added stories and sayings from elsewhere, and each of them put their material together in slightly different orders. So the usual view is that Mark's gospel was written around AD 65-70, with the other two about fifteen or twenty years later. If we ask where Mark got his material from, the answer the scholars will give is that all the stories about Jesus and his sayings circulated around the churches and were told and retold in the congregations before they got to be written down. Needless to say there are scholars whose life's work has been to explore the process of how our gospels reached us.

After the gospels comes the Acts of the Apostles, also by Luke, to carry on the story of Christianity from where his first book ended [see Acts 1:1].

Most of the rest of the New Testament is taken up by letters written by one or other of the apostles, with the apostle Paul being the most prolific. Why did they "write?" Sometimes Paul wrote because he was asked for advice, for example 1 Corinthians 7-8 were penned because the Corinthians had written to him for guidance on several matters [see 1 Corinthians 7:1]. Sometimes he wrote because he had advice to give, or errors to correct and issues to sort out, or thanks and encouragement to give to the churches he had founded. It looks as if Paul and the other leaders wrote letters for much the same reasons that John Wesley wrote letters in the early days of Methodism, because they couldn't be everywhere at once and letters were the best way of keeping in touch with and giving oversight to their churches and their assistants. But even here we must be careful. When I write a letter I check it, revise it and correct it before I send it, and my word-processor helps me to do it. Paul wrote next to nothing himself but dictated his letters to a secretary. The New Testament letters were spoken rather than written and revised.

Some of the letters are very detailed and give precise instructions about individuals or rulings on specific questions, but even then there are limits. For example on some issues Paul can say what Jesus thinks about it and that is the end of the matter [as in 1 Corinthians 7:10], and on others he gives his own advice which he knows that his readers will not necessarily take [as in 1 Corinthians 7 verses 12 and 17]. Other letters are more like theological manifestos setting out a major doctrinal issue. The two best examples of this are Paul's letter to the Romans and the anonymous letter to the Hebrews. But in every case the writer is a church leader writing to his churches. Sometimes the writers have to justify themselves or defend themselves, sometimes they have to insist on being heard, sometimes they quote what they have learned from someone else, sometimes they explain, sometimes they argue and even shout, sometimes they plead and appeal. Obviously these letters were valued for they were collected and preserved. In 2 Peter 3:15-16 we read this comment about Paul's letters,

> *"So also our beloved brother Paul wrote to you according to the wisdom given him, speaking of this as he does in all his letters. There are some things in them hard to understand, which the ignorant and unstable twist to their own destruction, as they do the other scriptures."*

From this we can see that by the time this letter was written [and it's usually thought of as being the last book of the New Testament to have been written, and not to have come from Peter himself] Paul's letters were being valued as part of the "scriptures" or special books. Even so the writer says simply that Paul wrote "according to the wisdom given him." Whether Paul himself would have been happy to have his letters valued as "scripture" is another question.

The New Testament closes with the Revelation to John, which claims to be a revelation from God through Jesus to an angel and then to John who faithfully wrote down all he had seen and heard in his vision, as he was told to do [Revelation 1:1-2, 21:5, 22:7-10].

At the end of this dash through the New Testament we should note that apart from the Book of Revelation there is nothing in the New Testament which claims to have been written at God's dictation. Of the two Gospel writers who tell us why they write one tells us of his hard work in gathering material and his careful attempt to get it right, and the other tells of selecting his material to make his point. The letters which make up a third of the New Testament show their writers struggling to find the best ways to express themselves and to convince their readers, and very rarely indeed do they say anything like the *"Thus says the Lord"* of the prophets. Here too I have not had time to go into much detail about how these New Testament books reached the form that we have them in today. All that I can say here is that the stories about Jesus were told and retold by preachers and teachers for years before they were written down, and his teachings were handed down in the same way.

The Bible is a precious gift to us, but it did not drop out of heaven. Much of it started out as spoken words, preached in sermons or told in stories. Then it was written. It was written by our forebears in the faith, some whose names we know and many we don't. So the <u>Methodist Catechism</u> puts it like this,

> *"The writers expressed themselves according to their own language, culture and point in history and in their different ways were all bearing witness to their faith in God."*

Brian Wren puts it beautifully in a new hymn,

> *"From Abraham to Nazareth*
> *The promise changed and grew,*
> *While some, remembering the past,*
> *Recorded what they knew,*
> *And some, in letters or laments,*
> *In prophecy and praise,*
> *Recovered, held and re-expressed*
> *New hope for changing days.*
>
> *For all the writings that survived,*
> *For leaders long ago,*
> *Who sifted, chose, and then preserved*
> *The Bible that we know,*
> *Give thanks...."*

[<u>Hymns and Psalms</u> 447, "Deep in the shadows of the past" by Brian A Wren (1936 -). Reprinted by permission of Oxford University Press]

8   Two sorts of details.

In the chapter before the last one we looked at how the churches selected some out of all of the writings that they possessed to go onto their official list of "Sacred Scripture." Or to put it another way, how the churches created The Bible or Bibles as we know them today from the large number of religious writings which they knew and valued. The writings which ended up on the Official List, in the Bible, were obviously cherished from the first time that they were read. Perhaps they were recognised as speaking with a special authority, or it was felt that they had the ring of truth about them. Perhaps the fact that the writer was an important church leader had something to do with it. Perhaps it was that they were so helpful to the ones who read them. Whatever it was only some of the letters and tracts written by the first Christians survived and only some of those were given the status of Holy Scripture.

In the last chapter we looked at how these books that were chosen came into being in the first place, at how and why they written and edited, and by whom. Christians believe that in the Bible we hear God speaking to us, but we have seen that the way that he speaks is through people, and the books of the Bible were written and produced by human beings like ourselves using their own minds, mouths and pens.

In this chapter I want to adopt the microscope approach and look at how the words and sentences arrived in those books. We have looked at the big question of who chose these books? We have looked at who wrote them and the sort of things they wrote. Now we come to the next question that we need to look at before we can make sensible comments on what the Bible is and isn't, and about how it can and should be used. So I have headed this microscope chapter "Two sorts of details," and in it I want to look at two things which can easily be overlooked or taken for granted. The first is, What shall we translate? The second is, How shall we translate it? The second question is obvious enough. I can best show what I mean by the first by using a hymn as an illustration. After that all my examples will be taken from the New Testament.

One of my *Desert Island Hymns* would have to be the great Holy Week hymn by Isaac Watts, "When I survey the wondrous cross." Let us imagine that a member of the Cornish Language Society wants to translate that hymn into Cornish. She looks up the hymn in <u>Hymns and Psalms</u>, reads it through, notices that a new verse has been put in which wasn't in the <u>Methodist Hymn Book</u>, and then stops at the fourth word in the second line of the last verse. This good Methodist has sung

"that were an <u>offering</u> far too small,"

all her life: but in the new book it says,

"that were a <u>present</u> far too small."

Which of these two words is she going to translate into Cornish? Let this incomer assume that there is a Cornish word for "offering" and another one for "present." So which does she use? That is what I mean by the question, What shall we translate? Obviously in this example the meanings of the two words are near enough: but which did Isaac Watts write? How come there are two different "texts" of this hymn? Which "text" should she translate?

We have many hundreds of "texts" of the New Testament, many hundreds of different manuscripts of parts or all of the New Testament, and they contain thousands of variations. Some of these are small ones like a different word or two as in the hymn, some are bigger differences. Before translators can translate the New Testament from its original Greek into English they have to work out which "text" or set of words they are going to translate. This is highly complicated work and "textual critics" devote their lives to poring over piles of manuscripts to try to decide what Paul or Matthew originally wrote, or to explain how these differences and variations arose.

So then to the first detail: What shall we

46

translate? Here are three examples of places where different New Testament manuscripts have different readings, so forcing the textual scholars to try to decide which, if any, was the original reading and which reading the translator should translate.

a) The beginning and the ending of the Gospel of Mark.

We'll start with the beginning because that is the simplest. In the NRSV the first verse of the gospel reads,

"The beginning of the good news of Jesus Christ, the Son of God."

But at the bottom of the page there is a note about this verse which says "Other ancient authorities lack *the Son of God*," which shows that we have some ancient manuscripts which do not include this phrase. Scholars have therefore had to weigh up the pros and cons and come to a conclusion about which of these variations they think is the original.

Turning to the end of Mark's gospel the NRSV stops at the odd ending, *".... they said nothing to anyone, for they were afraid."* Then there are two sentences in brackets called "The Shorter Ending of Mark" and then verses 9-20 are printed under the heading of "The Longer Ending of Mark." The note at that point explains what is going on, and I will quote it in full,

> *"Some of the most ancient authorities bring the book to a close at the end of verse 8. One authority concludes the book with the shorter ending; others include the shorter ending and then continue with verses 9-20. In most authorities verses 9-20 follow immediately after verse 8, though in some of these authorities the passage is marked as being doubtful."*

Even the *New International Version*, which no one can accuse of being a liberal translation, draws a line after *"they were afraid."* It then says in brackets that *"The two most reliable early manuscripts do not have Mark 16:9-20"* before it prints them. How and where the Gospel of Mark should end is therefore quite a mystery.

b) The story of the woman taken in adultery with its marvellous line about the one who is without sin throwing the first stone must be one of the best known stories about Jesus. But in the NRSV it is put in brackets with the note that,

> "The most ancient authorities lack [John] 7:53-8:11; other authorities add the passage here or after 7:36 or after 21:25 or after Luke 21:38, with variations of text; some mark the passage as doubtful."

Likewise the *New International Version* also brackets it off with the words, "The earliest and most reliable manuscripts do not have John 7:53-8:11." If the story is not in the earliest and most reliable manuscripts should we allow it to stay in our New Testaments? An interesting question.

c) I'm going to get around to the Black Pudding Question in a few pages' time. The discussion about it is found in Acts 15:20 and 15:29 which is repeated in Acts 21:25. These verses give the decision made by the Council of Jerusalem about which parts of the Jewish Law are no longer binding on Gentile converts to Christianity and which are still binding. In Acts 15:28-29 we read that the decision was this,

> "For it has seemed good to the Holy Spirit and to us to impose on you no further burden than these essentials: that you abstain from what has been sacrificed to idols and from blood and from what is strangled and from fornication."

But what I am quoting this for here is that in every one of these three places where that decision is quoted the NRSV has a note which says that "O*ther ancient authorities lack*" any reference to strangling! What the NRSV does not say is that this set of manuscripts not only omitted the reference to not eating meat from animals which had been killed by strangling, but also added at the two places in Acts 15 a much more wide-ranging, and to us a much more sensible, command that,

> *"whatever you do not wish to be done to you, do not do to others."*

So even when it came to reporting what was probably the most important issue the early church had to debate, the one about how much of the Jewish Law the Gentile Christians were to be expected to keep, the manuscripts of the Acts of the Apostles give significantly different versions of the decision!

These are only three examples out of many. Just how many is beyond counting. I started flicking through my new NRSV, which only gives the most important examples, but gave up after I had counted 72 notes in the margin which said that "Other ancient authorities read or add or lack..." and that was only in Matthew's gospel. My Greek New Testament goes into much more detail, and on average it has 25 lines of New Testament on each page, plus half a dozen lines of textual notes at the bottom of each page listing all the variations in the old manuscripts.

All this goes to show that the original text that Paul or Luke wrote is impossible to recover - the detectives can only make deductions, and we have to be grateful for their patience and skill. That much is widely agreed. A second conclusion, much more controversial but based on the evidence, would appear to be that no one in the early centuries of the church's life thought that the New Testament writings were to be preserved word for word and down to the last dot and comma. Instead they felt able to treat the manuscripts quite freely, expanding bits here and there, altering others, and making additions and subtractions. Not only that, some of the copyists were downright careless.

So on to the second detail: How shall we translate it? I am not talking here about simple translation questions like, Is the first line of the popular German carol "Stille Nacht, heilige Nacht" best translated by "Silent night, holy night" as in <u>Hymns and Psalms</u> or by "Still the night, holy the night" as in the <u>Methodist Hymn Book?</u> That is a question of style or taste, and opinions will differ, for both translations put over what the original means. No. Here I am talking about either not knowing what the original means at all, or about what to do when the original can be translated in different and conflicting ways. Here are some examples from the New Testament.

a) In the Lord's Prayer we are used to saying, *"Give us this day our daily bread."* But the meaning of the word translated *"daily"* is far from certain. It can also be translated as *"for tomorrow"* as the note in the NRSV at Matthew 6:11 and Luke 11:3 shows, but that too is little more than an educated guess.

b) The New Testament teaches clearly that Jesus is the Messiah or the Christ, that he is Lord and that he is the Son of God. Whether it ever says bluntly that Jesus is God is debatable, and one of the verses to debate over is Romans 9:5 which according to the NRSV can be translated in at least three different ways which give very different answers to the question. The translation given on the main page of the NRSV is

> "... and from them [that is, from the Israelites], according to the flesh, comes the Messiah, who is over all, God blessed for ever. Amen."

In the notes at the bottom of the page two other possible translations are given,

> "... and from them [that is, from the Israelites], according to the flesh, comes the Messiah, who is God over all, blessed for ever. Amen."

and

> "... and from them [that is, from the Israelites], according to the flesh, comes the Messiah. May he who is God over all be blessed for ever. Amen."

The first is ambiguous, the second says that Jesus is God, the third says that he isn't. Each of these is a reasonable translation of the Greek - which is the proper translation is an impossible question to answer.

c) Exactly the same problem on the same issue is found at Titus 2:13. On the page the NRSV reads,

> "... while we wait for the blessed hope and the manifestation of the glory of our great God and Saviour, Jesus Christ,"

which says that Jesus is God. In a note at the bottom is another equally possible translation which says he isn't,

> "... while we wait for the blessed hope and the manifestation of the glory of the great God and our Saviour, Jesus Christ."

d) Leaving heavy theology aside how should we behave? Should we *"associate with the lowly"* or *"give ourselves to humble tasks?"* Both are fair translations of Paul's instruction in Romans 12:16.

e) I end with a passage we have looked at before. What is the meaning of 2 Timothy 3:16? Is it,

> *"All scripture is inspired by God and is useful for teaching, for reproof, for correction, and for training in righteousness, so that everyone who belongs to God may be proficient, equipped for every good work?"*

Or is it the translation in the note at the bottom of the page,

> *"Every scripture inspired by God is also useful for teaching, for reproof, for correction, and for training in righteousness, so that everyone who belongs to God may be proficient, equipped for every good work?"*

For they don't mean the same thing do they?

These translation problems all come from the New Testament. Such problems are much more frequent in the Old Testament, where the note "Hebrew obscure" or "The meaning of the Hebrew is uncertain" occurs frequently in the footnotes of the NRSV.

In conclusion we have to admit that the existence of variations in different manuscripts of the books of our Bible is a fact. Different ways of translating the same sentence is also a fact. Manuscripts differ for all sorts of reasons, a copyist made a mistake, a copyist added an explanation, a copyist changed what he was copying because it didn't look right or he didn't agree with it! Here again is the human element. Where translators have to choose between opposite ways of translating the same words, how do they it? Here again is the human element.

When you are reading your Bible keep an eye on the footnotes or the margin for variant readings and different ways of translating things. The Bible is full of them, and they are often fascinating. But I have looked at a few of them in this chapter for a different reason, because these two facts are important in the wider issue we are looking at. They are pieces in the jigsaw of what the Bible is, and these two simple facts need to be taken into account before we can try to come to any conclusions at all about the inspiration and authority of the Bible.

It is to that important question that we must now turn.

9   So what can we say about the authority and inspiration of the Bible?

In this chapter we have reached the point where we can try to make a statement about the authority and inspiration of the Bible, which will take seriously the Bible as it is and the facts of how it has come to us.

First let me recap on what we have seen in the last four chapters. We have looked carefully at the Bible as it is and how it came to us and have made some important observations:

1   *that the Bible is not infallible,*

2   *that the Church created the Bible,*

3   *that the Bible was written by human authors and*

4   *that we cannot always get back to what those authors wrote or meant.*

We have seen that it is wrong to think that

> "The Bible is the dictated word of God, containing no errors, and everything in it is literally true."

We have seen that the Bible is not a magic book where every word, dot and comma has been put where it is by God. It contradicts itself at times and so it obviously contains mistakes or errors. On the other hand those who edited the Bible didn't try to disguise the contradictions and were prepared to live with the Bible as we have it, errors included. We have seen that we must also be prepared to live with a lot of variations in the ancient manuscripts and the knowledge that sometimes we do not know the meanings of the ancient words.

We have also seen that it is wrong to think that

> *"The Bible is the fallible product of human beings and must be given no more authority than any other book written."*

We have seen that the Bible is not something that Christians can simply take or leave as they feel like it. The ancient churches drew up their official lists of those books which they regarded as special because the books themselves obviously contained something which they thought was special. We have the Bibles that we do today because our forebears in the church valued and chose these 66 or so books to be on the official list and rejected the others.

We have seen that although the Bible was produced by the likes of you and me, by people who spoke with real voices and who wrote at particular times and in particular places for particular reasons, those who read it also heard God speaking through it. Presumably the writers said and wrote what they believed was true, and some went so far as to say explicitly that they were speaking and writing what God wanted to be said or written, and that is what the church of old heard. So the Bible that we have is a library of human books in which the church down the years has believed that the voice of God comes to us through the words of human beings.

All of this goes to show that the <u>Methodist Catechism</u> has got it about right when it says what it does about the Bible,

> *The Bible, comprising the Old and New Testaments, is the collection of books, gradually compiled, in which it is recorded how God has acted among, and spoken to and through, his people. The writers expressed themselves according to their own language, culture and point in history and in their different ways were all bearing witness to their faith in God. The Bible is the record of God's self-revelation, supremely in Jesus Christ, and is a means through which he still reveals himself, by the Holy Spirit.*

I write as one who believes most passionately in the inspiration of the Scriptures. I believe that the Bible is both inspired and inspiring. And I suspect that there are very few of you who are reading this who do not share that belief. So when I talk about the inspiration of the Bible I mean that it is able to inspire me in all kinds of ways in my Christian faith and pilgrimage today. I believe that the reason that it can do this is that it comes from God. I want to assert that the Bible speaks to us of God and that it comes to us from God.

It has not, as we have seen, come to us directly from God. It was written by human hands, edited with human eyes; its shape and content has been decided by human minds, even by people sitting in committees. It certainly comes to us copied, printed, transported and sold by human beings. Yet I still want to say, as has been said by so many in the past, that the ultimate source of the Bible is God. He is the one who inspired the writers with visions of his truth, intimations of his glory, awareness of his power, convictions about his deeds, beliefs about his nature, and understandings of his will and his ways. So I want to say that the Bible is the Word of God. I want to affirm that the Bible's source is in God.

If we ask the questions, How has God spoken this Word? How has this Word come to us? How is the Bible inspired? Then our answer must take into account the Bible as it is and as we have seen it to be. Our answer must take into account such facts as the Bible's errors and contradictions, and such facts as its diversity of authorship and complicated editorial work. Do such facts as these invalidate the idea that the Bible is inspired by God? They do not do so to me. They do force me to ask however, that if the Bible as we have it is the result of God's inspiration then how does God's inspiration *work*? What I am insisting on is that we must start from the Bible as it is, including its contradictions, inconsistencies and mistakes, and then go on to work out our theory of its inspiration which takes all that fully into account.

I write this as a Methodist minister who has been "called to preach" and as one who believes that preaching is important. I know that much preaching is dull, tedious and boring, to use the favourite word of today's young, for I have spent a lot of the last four years sitting in pews listening to it. But for all that I still believe in preaching, and I wish that Methodist preachers, both ministers and Local Preachers, would take it more seriously and take every opportunity and make every effort to learn to do it better. What has that got to do with the inspiration of the Bible? I hear you muttering at this point. Simply this. I suggest that preaching provides a very good model for a workable theory of the inspiration of the Bible.

Begin from your own experience. Every Sunday I hope that most of you either sit in church and listen to a sermon, or stand in a pulpit and preach one as I do. I believe that what I am doing there is speaking the Word of God to his people by the inspiration of his Spirit. If I thought it was otherwise I would not dare enter a pulpit. I am not giving my own opinions on this, that or the other religious topic: but a message which I believe God has for his people. It is quite obvious that my ideas and words are being used, as are my voice and my mannerisms. It is equally obvious that I am a much poorer medium for God's Spirit that Isaiah or Paul were, or than John Wesley or Cardinal Newman or David Watson: but the difference is one of degree, not of kind. Surely that is inspiration, the human spirit opened up to God so that he can communicate through it? In so doing he uses the thoughts, feelings, attitudes and experiences of the person concerned, and these are reflected in the end product, but so is his message. To put it another way, God's word is always incarnate, embodied, and the character of the messenger is always there: but it is still God's word which is embodied, inspired and revealing his will. That, it seems to me, is how inspiration works, and that is how we can think of the inspiration of the Bible in a way which takes the facts of the Bible seriously as well as enabling us to listen to its message with every attention and all seriousness.

I write as one who also believes firmly in the authority of the Bible. The Methodist <u>Deed of Union</u> says that the Bible records God's revelation, and that this revelation is our *"supreme rule of faith and practice."* It does not say that every dot and comma of the Bible itself is God's revelation, nor that the Bible itself is our supreme authority. But it says enough to make it plain that the Bible is important, and that what it says in matters of belief and behaviour is to be listened to very carefully indeed. I learned this as a teenager in our little chapel at Horsehay in Shropshire where in peeling paint above the pulpit there were the words from Psalm 119, *"Thy Word is a Lamp unto my Feet."* So, *What does the Bible say?* is for me one of the most important questions to ask in working out what we ought to do or think on any issue.

But that is not as simple a question as it looks, as we began to see in the discussion about Women Preachers in chapter 2. Trying to answer it must take into account the Bible as it is and as we have seen it to be. Our answer to this question must take into account such facts as the Bible's errors and contradictions, and such facts as its diversity of authorship and complicated editorial work. Some people go so far as to say that such facts as these mean that the Bible cannot be used to give authoritative answers to today's questions. I do not agree. Perhaps the model of preaching is helpful here also. We take careful note of what preachers say, and are ready to be taught or challenged or guided by it. But we do not believe or do everything that preachers say just because they say it. We recognise that they believe in what they are saying, and that they believe that God has given them that message for us today: but we know that sometimes they are biased and have a few bees in their bonnets. Or that sometimes they haven't had time to prepare properly. We also know that sometimes they don't really know what they are talking about. So we listen carefully, think about it, talk to others about it, read about it and try to come to a considered conclusion. Sometimes we will conclude that the preacher was one hundred per cent right, occasionally we will think that she got it completely wrong: but mostly we will be grateful for the help and guidance given. Perhaps the authority of the Bible is like that of the preacher, only more so?

The time has nearly come to talk about Black Pudding.

10 Divorce, Black Pudding and other things.

The time has come, nearly, to talk about Black Pudding. But first I want to talk about divorce. After Black Pudding I shall talk about other things.

But why are we looking at these things at all? Perhaps a brief recap might help. This is a book about the Bible and the use of the Bible in the Methodist Church. So far I have spent a lot of time looking at what the Bible is, at how it came to us, at what the Bible writers thought they were doing, as far as they tell us, and at how we got the Bible we use. I have shown, I hope, that the Bible is a human book marked by the views of its different authors, and marked too by errors and inconsistencies. I have also shown, I hope, that it is a special book, valued by the Church, as a way in which we hear God speaking to us, albeit through the voices of some very human characters.

I have been looking at the Bible in this way because there is a big debate going on in the Methodist Church today, and in other churches as well, about the authority that the Bible has or should have for the Church and the Christian. That is what we are going to begin to look at in this chapter. How should we and how do we use the Bible in the Methodist Church? In questions about right and wrong do we simply accept what the Bible says? Do we believe that the Bible can teach us about right and wrong? Do we think that if the Bible says something about morals, then what it says has to be obeyed whether we like it or not? Does the Bible have the final say, for Methodists and the Methodist Church, in matters of right and wrong? Should it? These are the questions I want to begin to look at in this chapter. All the examples which we will look at now concern specific commands or statements in the New Testament.

Let us begin with divorce. The Methodist Church accepts divorce and permits the remarriage in church of people who have been divorced. Obviously we would prefer it if divorce was never necessary. Life would be much better if every married couple could live together in harmony until death did them part: but life is not like that. Marriages go wrong and divorces happen, and the Methodist Church accepts that they do. Some churches do not recognise divorce and therefore do not allow divorced people to remarry in church. The Roman Catholic Church is logical and consistent in taking this stance - it does not recognise divorce, and so it does not allow divorced people to remarry in church. If they do remarry in a Registry Office or anywhere else they cannot take communion any more. The Church of England is very sticky about allowing divorced people to remarry in church but it does offer a service of blessing to people who have remarried in a Registry Office. Personally the logic of that escapes me, and it looks to me very much like the nonsense of the Princess Royal disappearing over the border to remarry and then being congratulated by the Archbishop of Canterbury. The Methodist Church recognises that divorce happens and offers divorcees a new start. We do not remarry divorcees willy-nilly, and the minister has to make sure that any divorced person wanting to remarry did not make the major contribution to the breakdown of their previous marriage, or that if they did they have learned their lesson and are coming this time with a better understanding of what marriage is all about. We offer a second, or even a third chance, presumably because we believe in a God who forgives and offers new starts. Methodist ministers are not obliged to remarry divorcees and those who in good conscience feel unable to do so do not have to do so. In every case the Chairman of the District has to be consulted. In statistical terms in my own ministry I have conducted two or three marriages involving divorcees to every one involving first-timers, and I think that my experience is quite typical. So that is what we do in the Methodist Church.

But what about the Bible? In the Old Testament divorce is allowed and so is remarriage after it, although one of the prophets gets hot under the collar about it. There was some controversy about grounds for divorce at the time of Jesus, and Jesus seems to have taken the hard line rather than the soft one, although the gospels do not agree on what he actually said on the subject. According to Matthew 5:32 Jesus says,

> "But I say to you that anyone who divorces his wife, except on the ground of unchastity, causes her to commit adultery; and whoever marries a divorced woman commits adultery."

According to Luke 16:18 he takes an even harder line,

> "Anyone who divorces his wife and marries another commits adultery, and whoever marries a woman divorced from her husband commits adultery."

According to both of these sayings of Jesus the remarriage of a divorced woman is adultery and therefore wrong. Yet the Methodist Church permits the remarriage of divorced women which is contrary to both of these sayings of Jesus in the New Testament, and the remarriage of divorced men which is contrary to the saying in Luke.

Why do we do it? Our latest report on A Christian Understanding of Family Life, the Single Person and Marriage, which was adopted at the 1992 Conference, devotes three short paragraphs to answering that question [on pages 23-24]. In a nutshell it says that there are hints in the New Testament that the hard line in Luke was not seen as the last word on the subject, and that in any case our world is in many ways far away from the world of the New Testament. In its final sentence it briefly touches on a different argument which I think is the crucial one. It does not spell it out, but it is the argument which says that forgiveness and new starts is one of the "big themes" of the New Testament, and must be given more weight in this instance than the teaching of one or two specific texts.

Whatever you think of these arguments it is a fact that on the question of the remarriage of divorced people the Methodist Church approves a practice which is forbidden by Jesus himself. Personally I do not feel bad about this in any way, and regard the remarriage of divorced people as an opportunity to show in a practical way the forgiveness of a God who is always trying to make us whole and to make all things new.

Now we come to Black Pudding. A case in which no Methodists known to me personally actually do what the Bible says.

Jesus was a Jew, and so were all the disciples and all the early Christians. Then Saul was converted and became Paul the Apostle to the Gentiles. As a result of Paul's missionary work gentiles, non-Jewish people, began to want to join the Church. So an urgent question arose: how much of the Jewish Law should gentile converts be expected to keep? Should the men be circumcised? Should they keep the laws about food? Should they go to the Temple and offer the proper sacrifices? Dispute on some of these issues was very bitter indeed. According to Acts 15 the apostles and elders of the Church met together to consider the matter, and they made a ruling on this urgent question. The ruling was suggested by James, Jesus's brother, and it was agreed that a letter should be sent to the gentile churches telling them of the decision. The decision was this,

> *"It has seemed good to the Holy Spirit and to us to impose on you no further burden than these essentials: that you abstain from what has been sacrificed to idols and from blood and from what has been strangled and from fornication."*

We read this in Acts 15:28-29, which is repeated in Acts 21:25. Note that this passage is talking about "essentials" and not options. Christians must avoid these four things. All the other Jewish food laws about clean and unclean animals do not have to be kept. Jesus himself had dismissed those food laws [see Mark 7:18-19], and Peter had been told the same thing in a vision [see Acts 10:9-16]. So the Christians could eat pork sausages, bacon sandwiches and hamburgers if they wanted to, for pork was now okay to eat. But on one condition, that when the pig was killed the blood from it was drained in the proper kosher way. Pork was now okay, but blood was not - the old blood commandment from Leviticus 7:26 and 17:10 was still to be obeyed. The ruling is clear. Acts 15:28-29 repeated in Acts 21:25 is a general rule applying to all Christians - *We should not eat blood*.

Yet I eat Black Pudding, fried for breakfast when my wife isn't looking, though I don't eat rare steaks because the sight of something oozing out when I cut them puts me right off [The steaks I enjoy are charcoal coloured]. But if I was to take the Bible literally both Black Pudding and rare steaks are forbidden. But I don't know any Methodists personally, or any other Christians either, who don't eat Black Pudding because of Acts 15. I know a lot of people who don't eat the stuff because they can't stand the taste of it or the thought of it, or because they are vegetarians for one reason or another, or who have just never thought of eating it because they've never tasted the real thing [modern supermarket black puddings are to real Black Puddings what sliced loaves in plastic bags are to bread]: but none who abstain because the Bible says so. But the Bible is plain and straightforward on this one as the Jehovah's Witnesses keep reminding us - yet we ignore it. Why?

The other ruling about food in Acts 15 was obviously controversial, which is presumably why a whole series of ancient manuscripts miss it out as we saw in chapter 8. That is the decision that Christians should not eat meat from animals which have been strangled. My gran had a chicken-run in the backyard, and every Christmas we had a cockerel that grampa, her dad, used to kill by wringing its neck. Grampa knew his Bible, for he had been a Methodist New Connexion Local Preacher since about 1898, but Acts 15 never stopped him killing the Christmas bird that way.

What about other things? The Methodist Church baptises infants, and Infant Baptism is one of my favourite services, though I don't like the service in the Methodist Service Book and I like the proposed new one even less. But there is not a shred of evidence in the New Testament that we ought to do any such thing and quite a bit which suggests we shouldn't. If a Bible was put in one of these space probes and it landed on Mars, and if the Martians read it and were converted and tried to set up a Church on the New Testament pattern, then there is no way that they would baptise their little

Martians.   Nor would they have Church Councils, Circuits, Ministers, organs, Collections, chapels, Hymn Books or Harvest Festivals either but I won't mention them.

What about Methodists in court? If you are called as a witness what do you do? Do you swear on the Bible or not? The Quakers used to make a big thing of this one on the basis of the saying of Jesus in Matthew 5:33-37 that swearing on oath was out and our "Yes" or "No" was to be enough. Swearing on the Bible or anything else is forbidden by Jesus. I've only ever been called as a witness once and in view of my dog collar the magistrate decided that I didn't need to swear on oath at all, but what should I have done if he hadn't? What do you do? Why?

We've already had a chapter on women preachers and women church leaders. The Bible is against them too, as we saw, though we have them.

So far my examples have been of things which the New Testament does not approve of but which Methodism practices. For an opposite sort of example take alcohol, or rather, Don't take alcohol! I am a teetotaller and have been since I was 17. I consider alcohol to be a drug of the same order as tobacco, marijuana and heroin. I do not see how any Christian who believes that his or her body is a temple of the Holy Spirit [as it says several times in the New Testament] can possibly take alcohol or any other drug. Yet the Bible is quite happy with it. Timothy is told to drink wine regularly for his health's sake [1 Timothy 5:23] and one of the pictures of God's kingdom come on earth is a picture of much eating and drinking. As for Jesus turning water into wine, I prefer to ignore that one. On this issue I and quite a number of Methodists do not approve of something which the New Testament is happy with.

Or what about the Use of Sunday? The New Testament says absolutely nothing about the Use of Sunday. It says quite a bit about the Sabbath, which is Saturday. The Jews worshipped on a Saturday, the Christians from quite early on seem to have worshipped like we do on a Sunday. Yet I can find nothing in the New Testament to justify the change. By whose authority do we worship on a day different from the one the Bible says? The Seventh Day Adventists stick to the letter of the Bible - they worship on the Sabbath, on Saturdays.

Fifty years ago the Church was bitterly divided over the question of war and peace. Could Christians go to war? Could Conscientious Objectors be Christians, or could real Christians be anything but Conscientious Objectors? Both sides claimed the support of the Bible. In particular the Conscientious Objectors could point to words of Jesus about loving one's enemies and not resisting evildoers, yet the majority of Christians were not convinced. In 1939 I would not have been convinced either.

Lastly, what about credit cards? Or about not paying the Assessment? St Paul forbids both of these in Romans 13:8.

In this chapter we have looked at a number of examples where the New Testament gives explicit commandments in one way or another about right and wrong. All of the examples I have given are of issues where the Bible says one thing and the Methodist Church or individual Methodists tend to do another, and my list was by no means a full one. Obviously there are many more examples of New Testament commands with which the Methodist Church and individual Methodists agree wholeheartedly, from the big ones about murder, theft or adultery to smaller ones about patience, envy or honesty. But divorce, Black Pudding and these other things all go to show that the Methodist Church and individual Methodists do not simply make up their minds on right and wrong by reading texts of Scripture. Perhaps we should: but we don't. That is a fact. We *interpret* the Bible, and in this process other things come into play in addition to what the Bible actually says. That this is all right and proper I will show in the next chapter.

11 Like a mobile.

How does the Methodist Church use the Bible? In the last chapter we looked at a number of examples of Methodist views on right and wrong which are at odds with sayings in the New Testament. On questions of right and wrong the Methodist Church and individual Methodists do not simply read a text of the New Testament and do precisely what it says. Sometimes they do that, but often they don't. I promised at the end of the last chapter to try to show next how this picking and choosing was above board and proper. If this is how the Methodist Church uses the Bible, how can such use be justified?

One answer might be that because the Bible itself does not always speak with one voice it is inevitable that we must compare and contrast different passages on the same topic and pick and choose between them. Another might be that in view of how the Bible came into being, through the fallible opinions and decisions of our faithful forebears, it is inevitable that we must weigh up each individual viewpoint and discuss it in the light of the teachings of the Bible as a whole. Another might be that the Bible as it is, obviously not a unified and systematic Handbook on Right and Wrong, makes using our own minds to examine it inevitable. Another might be that as the Church created the Bible, with the guidance and help of God in the process, so the Church today has the right and the duty to interpret the Bible for today, also with the help and guidance of God in the process. Another might be that everyone and every church, whether they admit it or not, picks and chooses - there is no other way.

To give a careful Methodist answer let me quote the only person since Methodist Union in 1932 who has been President of the Conference twice, Rev Dr Donald English. In 1985 the Home Mission Division of the Methodist Church, under his leadership, produced a very important report called "<u>Sharing in God's Mission.</u>" The aim of this report was to get every church and circuit in the country to look at what it was doing and to ask what it ought to be doing. The basic conviction of the report was that God is a God of love and that he is at work in his world. It follows that our mission is to share in what God is doing or wanting to be done, and the report itself asked questions and made suggestions for churches and circuits to think about, as well as for individuals, so that we could share in God's mission where we were. The Home Mission Division produced a tape to accompany the report, and a popular version of the report and the tape are still available from the Publishing House. Both are very well worth having. The first talk on the tape is about God and about how we know anything about him, and in its answer is the answer to our question in this chapter. Donald English says this,

> "As Christians we gain our knowledge of God from the Bible in general and Jesus Christ in particular, a knowledge which has been and continues to be tested through our Christian traditions down the ages, in the exercise of God-given reason and in our personal experience of living in the world according to our faith."

Here Dr English mentions four things which need to be kept in mind when we talk about God's will and his ways: Scripture, Tradition, Reason and Experience. He then goes on to say that these *"sources of knowledge,"* as he calls these four things, can be likened to a child's mobile moving gently and gracefully round and round in a breeze. The main centrepiece is the Bible, which for John Wesley, our founder,

> *"was the centrepiece for our knowledge of God through Jesus Christ by the Holy Spirit. Revolving around the outside as supporting pieces in the mobile are Reason, Tradition and Experience. As you watch the mobile you will always find the Bible in the centre, but you are looking at it through the perspective of Tradition, or Reason, or Experience at any given moment. At the same time they receive their perspective and retain their position in*

relation to the Bible, it remains central."

He concludes that this was, and is,

> *"quite literally a mobile way of doing theology. The centrality of the Biblical message was maintained yet Reason, Tradition and Experience had their proper places. All three were used in the attempt to understand the Bible, yet all three were constantly examined, tested and verified or qualified according to the Bible as different questions arose and solutions were offered."*

In this mobile theology the teaching of the Bible is in the centre. But when we read the Bible we read it from where we are now as Christian people in today's church ["Experience"]. We read it as heirs of a long tradition of looking at the Bible and learning other things of God's will and his ways over the centuries ["Tradition"]. We read it as people who bring all of the truth that comes through education and science to bear on any given question ["Reason"]. We read it also as people who believe that God's Spirit is active in our own lives and in the life of the church today, guiding and leading us on as Jesus promised that he would [John 14:26, 16:13 - more "Experience"]. At any given moment or on any particular question we will examine the Bible teaching from these other three perspectives, as well as looking carefully at the teaching of other parts of the Bible to see if these have any bearing on the issues to hand. But equally, as Dr English said, we will also look hard at our own experience, or the traditions of the Church, or our own arguing and reasoning in the light of the Bible, for the Bible must inform these things as well as be informed by them. All of this is involved in the process of looking at what a particular text or passage from the Bible has to say to us today. To see what a particular text or passage from the Bible has to say to us today is therefore no easy or straightforward task.

Let us assume that we want to look at a Bible passage about a moral issue. To do it begins with a very careful look at the passage itself - we study its wording and the meaning of the words used, then we look at its historical context and where it is found in the Bible itself, at who wrote it and when, so that we can see what it might have meant to the people who heard it in the first place. We will then try to see where this passage fits in with other similar passages or verses, and how it fits in with more general ideas or themes from the Bible. An old way of putting this is to say that "Scripture must interpret Scripture," because it is so easy to lift a verse out of its context and make it mean what you want it to mean. So a control and safeguard against this is to "compare Scripture with Scripture." Next we should look at how our Christian forebears down the years have understood the passage or what they have thought about the issue, especially perhaps the Early Fathers, the great Reformers or our own Methodist ancestors from JW onwards. We will also look at whatever insight modern knowledge has to throw on the question at hand, together with what our fellow Christians think about it today. We will pray about the question and look for the guidance of God's Spirit. We would do all of this as thoroughly, carefully and prayerfully as we could, and then come to a conclusion. Such is the process of understanding or interpreting the Bible.

This is what every Preacher does every Sunday with every text or theme that they preach about, or at least it ought to be.

This is what every Christian does, even though they don't perhaps realise that they are doing some of it, when they decide that its okay after all to swear on oath as a witness, or to eat Black Pudding or, for the women only, not to wear a hat when they go to church next. All of these decisions involve interpreting the Bible. We all do it, one way or another. Every time we read the Bible we interpret what we read. We filter it through our minds, hearts and lives. We ask, "What has this to say to me?" or "What has this to say to us?" And asking those questions is beginning the process of interpretation.

This is what the Methodist Church tries to do when from time to time it is asked to make a ruling on a particular moral issue. It follows this procedure and tries to come to a common mind, because one of the dangers in interpreting the Bible has always been that individuals can get it wrong. I'm sure that all of us have heard sermons where Preachers have come up with something very odd indeed from the texts that they were using. There is a warning note about that in the New Testament itself. In 2 Peter 1:20 we read this,

> *"First of all you must understand this, that no prophecy of scripture is a matter of one's own interpretation."*

This verse is about understanding prophecies in the Bible, but it surely applies to other things too when it says that trying to understand particular passages in the Bible is something that is better done together than privately. Churches can get it wrong as well of course, but discussion helps to prevent it.

Finally let me quote again from the <u>Methodist Catechism</u>, which has a relevant question. In the answer you can see the four elements of Scripture, Tradition, Reason and Experience intertwined and influencing each other:

<u>Question 24: How does God guide us?</u>

> *God guides us from within, through the Holy Spirit's prompting of our conscience. He guides us through the Bible, as we study its teaching. He guides us through Christian fellowship, the advice of friends, and as we respond to daily events and circumstances. He guides us particularly as we seek to be imitators of Jesus Christ.*

It was by using this "mobile method" of doing theology that the Conference Commission on Human Sexuality produced its report on Human Sexuality in 1990. This report is coming up for decision at the Conference in Derby in June, and this is the report which has aroused so much controversy in certain quarters. To that report we must now turn.

12   The Human Sexuality Report.

All the mainline churches in Britain have had discussion of human sexuality on their agendas in one way or another since the 1970's. The Methodist Conference first looked at some of the modern issues in 1976 and a report was produced in 1979, though it was put on ice by the Conference of 1982 which concluded that *"no definitive judgement was yet possible,"* to quote from paragraph 26 of the new report. The present report was commissioned in 1988, presented in 1990 and comes to the Conference in Derby this summer for decision. It is a wide-ranging report which covers many aspects of human sexuality, and its title is the <u>Report of the Commission on Human Sexuality</u>, but because the controversy about it centres on its discussion of homosexuality it is sometimes called the *"Homosexuality* Report" by mistake.

One of the seven terms of reference given to the Commission was *"to make recommendations, as to personal lifestyle and corporate discipline, with reference to both members and those who hold office in the Church"* [paragraph 11]. In particular in this area the report looks at whether or not the Methodist Church should accept as candidates for the ministry people of homosexual orientation or homosexual practice. The answer to that question will also have implications for all who hold office in the Methodist Church, and for all who are members of it. The position at present is that we have no ruling on the question [paragraph 184], and the report concludes with the recommendation that for now we leave it that way [paragraphs 185 and 186].

I will outline the report in a moment. After that I do not intend to discuss the report itself in general or any of the questions it looks at about human sexuality. The Conference asked Districts, Circuits, local churches and individuals to do that eighteen months ago, and produced a study pack to accompany the report to help that happen. What I do intend to do in the rest of this chapter is to look at the report and the Bible, because some people are attacking the report on the grounds that it accepts some sexual practices which the Bible forbids. And there is no doubt at all that the Bible does condemn genital sexual acts between people of the same sex. The question is, almost needless to say by this point in the book I hope, Does that mean that we should also utterly oppose such practices? The report answers - Not necessarily. And that is where some of the controversy lies. Some see the report as a test case on where Methodism stands on the Bible. If, What authority does the Bible have for us? is the question, they accuse the report of giving the answer - Not very much.

The outline of the report is this:

> Introduction: paragraphs 1-12
> Human Sexuality as a Source of Joy: 13-24
> Changes in Church and Society: 25-37
> Varieties of Life Style in Methodism: 38-80
> The Biblical Material:
>   Introduction: Approaching Scripture 81-100
>   The Old Testament: 101-111
>   The New Testament: 112-116
>   Conclusions: 117-126
> Sociological Studies: 127-132
> Biological Studies: 133-142
> Psychological Studies: 143-147
> Conclusions to these three: 148-150
> Corporate Life and Institutional Decisions:
>   151-179
> Conclusion: 180-187

From this you can see that space is given to a discussion of the teaching of the Bible [paragraphs 81 to 126], and you can also see that Reason [Sociological, Biological and Psychological studies, paragraphs 127 to 147] and Experience ["Varieties of Life style in Methodism", paragraphs 38 to 80] are also used to examine the whole question. Tradition doesn't get too much explicit mention. The report is a conversation between those three "sources of knowledge," each influencing the other, with the Bible as the centrepiece. Where it becomes controversial is that in the end the report refuses to repeat the Bible's clear condemnation of certain genital sexual acts between people of the same sex, and leaves open the question of such activities in gay partnerships. How does it reach this conclusion?

The specific discussion of the Biblical material in the report is in four parts:

1. In the introduction, *"Approaching Scripture,"* the report notes that as each of us reads the Bible we do so with our own questions and outlook to see what it has to say to us. It observes that we interpret the Bible in different ways and we do not necessarily reach the same conclusions. It says that the Bible is a huge and complicated book which itself does not speak with one voice. It points out that the Bible is an ancient book written over many hundreds of years in several different ancient cultures and situations. It accepts that there is sometimes a conflict between specific verses and general themes. It agrees that the process of interpreting the Bible is an ongoing task which the Church is engaged in all the time. It also admits that while all the members of the Commission agreed on the need to discover the mind of Scripture on the questions of human sexuality, they did not all agree on how much weight in the end should be given to what the Bible said.

The introduction says that they looked first at Bible views on human sexuality in broad terms and then at key texts and passages in detail. In the New Testament the central note is that God's will and his ways are seen clearest of all in the life and teaching, death and resurrection of Jesus. Here "love" and "acceptance" are two key words - Jesus's life of love towards God and everyone he encountered, and his acceptance of all sorts and conditions of people with an invitation to them to change their ways and follow him. The introduction notes that the early Christian churches had to struggle in different ways to work out what the story of Jesus meant for them in their different settings. In the Old Testament our human life is set in the framework of God's good creation, and so our sexuality is a gift to be enjoyed and cherished. But the Old Testament is also aware of how life can be spoilt and abused, and so it tries to protect the vulnerable and safeguard human values by rules and regulations. The Bible, it concludes, shows us both sides of human life - the good and the bad, the ideal and the real, the dream and the nightmare.

2. The Old Testament discussion concentrates on homosexuality, and in particular notes that in the laws in Leviticus male homosexual genital acts are unambiguously condemned [Leviticus 18:22 and 20:13 are the particular verses].

At this point the report points out that lots of other things are equally condemned in those laws, such as wearing clothes made out of two kinds of fabrics and the eating of meat with the blood in it [there's that Black Pudding again]. So it asks the question, *"Does the fact that the Levitical law against homosexuality is found with such a series of timebound localised regulations limit its application?"* It then asserts that we have to distinguish between "ceremonial" and "moral" laws, and says that that is not always easy either. It ends that paragraph [paragraph 106] by saying that the debate about the place of the Leviticus purity laws will go on.

The Old Testament section ends by asking if these specific texts should have the last word? Might there be *"deeper biblical principles"* in the Old Testament itself? Might the moral issue of homosexuality need *"to be reinterpreted in the light of the underlying message of the Bible, especially the New Testament?"*

3. The New Testament section is very short because it refers to a detailed study of the New Testament passages about homosexuality submitted to Conference in 1980 as a supplement to the previous report. The three passages concerned are all in letters of Paul [1 Corinthians 6:9-11, Romans 1:26-27 and 1 Timothy 1:8-11] and show that Paul rejects homosexual practice. The sentence at the end notes that it does not look as if Paul *"knows of an exclusively orientated homosexual condition."*

4. The conclusion to the Biblical section begins with the general observation that *"it is safe to conclude that the burden of biblical evidence is to reject homosexuality."*

Next it notes something that the Sunday papers would do well to note, that in the Bible sexual sins are given less prominence than others such as strife, greed, and idolatry. It also notes that some expressions of homosexuality known to us today are unmentioned in the Bible.

Next it says that we cannot simply dismiss all the sexual laws of the Bible as being conditioned by an ancient culture different from ours and therefore irrelevant to us in our different culture. Of course they are culturally conditioned, what else could they be if the Bible was written in the way that it was? But we still have to read these laws and ask how God is speaking to us through them. And that, as we have seen, is where different opinions are possible because we weigh the various factors involved differently.

Then it notes that we have to decide on how much of the Jewish law still applies for Christians, and that Paul and the Bible do not throw the baby out with the bathwater here. There are still rules and regulations, laws and boundaries in the Christian Faith. As Christians we are not free to do as we please.

Next it repeats the statement that although the Bible condemns homosexuality it is not precisely clear what is being condemned. Is Paul condemning the corruption associated with homosexuality in his day as in ours - the exploitation of boys, sex for sale, promiscuity, sexual violence? If he is we would all agree that he is right to do so. But what of those other expressions of homosexuality which involve tenderness, affection and fidelity in stable and committed relationships? We do not know.

The conclusion to the Biblical section ends by saying that although some of the Bible texts are unambiguous, they might not be the final answer, because for us the Bible is in dialogue with contemporary society, and reading the Bible is *"always about discerning the presence and purpose of God in contemporary society."* So the discussion moves on to sociological studies.

As I said at the beginning of the chapter the whole

report ends by recommending that we should not make any ruling on the question of members of the Methodist Church and homosexuality in general or the practice of homosexual genital sexual acts in gay or lesbian partnerships. It reaches this conclusion after looking at the issue from all angles, and recognising that it is a very complicated issue. The report says that in this and in much else we are *"seeking after truth, wrestling with Scripture, trying to understand God's world .... and all the time we are struggling to see through a glass darkly"* [paragraph 180]. Some supporters of the report recognise that the Bible is quite specifically opposed to homosexual genital sexual acts, but then say that taking all other things into account it is possible to come to a different opinion. Other supporters conclude that at the moment we must be neutral on the question of homosexual sexual acts. Others say that we should accept gay partnerships and that what goes on in bed within stable and committed relationships is the business of no one but the couple concerned. Each group could make out a case for their statement from the Bible, though we would not all find them convincing. Others supporters believe that homosexual genital acts are wrong but that legislation about them is also wrong. Opponents of the report are as varied as its supporters, but many say that the Methodist Church should not leave open a question to which the Bible gives a clear negative answer, and in so doing give tacit approval to what the Bible so clearly forbids.

This brief look at the report has shown, I hope, that the Human Sexuality Report follows the same method of working out what Methodism believes on this, that or the other issue which we have seen at work explicitly or implicitly in the examples discussed in chapter 10. Not every Methodist agrees with our official position on divorce, and there are some Methodist chapels where a woman is not welcome in the pulpit: but there has not been an outcry about Methodism no longer believing the Bible because of its divorce rules or its use of women preachers or ministers although that is the outcry in some quarters about this report. Partly this is because sexuality is such an emotive topic, and because homosexuality is a subject which arouses all kinds of emotions and feelings which I am in no way competent to understand or explain. But partly it is because this question is an urgent one for our generation, and in an age which seems to need clear statements of right and wrong many Christians feel threatened when the authority of the Bible on this vital question seems to be ignored so blatantly, and so all of the Bible's authority seems to be put in jeopardy.

A friend of mine puts his objection to the report like this, that the report just goes too far. He argues that he can just about see that there is enough in the New Testament to allow us to remarry divorced people despite the fact that there are some very clear New Testament prohibitions against doing it. The same is true about women preachers, he says. But he argues that there is absolutely nothing in the Bible which shows that we could allow gay partnerships. This particular report and its recommendation just goes too far. But my question to my friend is, How do we measure what is too far? Is the eating of blood products going too far? The Jehovah's Witnesses would say yes it is. Is worshipping on a Sunday rather than on the Sabbath going too far? The Seventh Day Adventists would say yes it is. Is remarrying divorced people in church going too far? The Church of England, officially at least, would say yes it is. Is permitting women to preach in church going too far? Some Independent Evangelical Churches would say yes it is. Is allowing women to appear in church without hats going too far? Some Black Churches in Birmingham would say yes it is. Is accepting Christian gay partnerships going too far? Some Methodists would say yes it is. But in all of these examples there are other equally convinced and sincere Christians who would say no, it is not going too far.

The reasons these other Christians will give for saying that approving this or that practice is not going too far will vary from issue to issue, and I have already given examples of some of the reasons in some of these issues in previous chapters. You will also know, if you think about it, your reasons for thinking that it is not going too far to allow women to go to chapel without a hat or whatever it is. The position we are in with the Human Sexuality report at the moment is that for some in all good conscience it just goes too far. For others in equally good conscience it does not.

In this chapter I am not arguing that we should be in favour of the Human Sexuality report and its conclusions, nor am I arguing that we should be against it. In fact I am keeping my opinion on the matter firmly to myself. What I am arguing here is that the report uses our traditional Methodist way of reasoning things out. It takes the Bible seriously but does not necessarily believe that specific Bible texts should always have the last word. You might argue that the report has got it wrong this time and that is this instance the Bible should have the last word. Or you might not. What I am saying is simply that you cannot accuse the Methodist Church of not taking the Bible seriously on this question. You might disagree with the report, but you cannot disagree with it just because it does not accept some specific commands in the Bible, or at least you can't if, for example, you yourself are a woman preacher or are a divorced person who has been remarried in church or if you eat Black Pudding. In the same way that you have justified those things you could, though I am not saying you should, justify the conclusions of the report.

When I quoted the Black Pudding rule to another of my friends who was saying that because the New Testament forbids homosexual sexual acts then we must forbid them as well, she shouted at me and told me not to be silly. She said that it is obvious to anyone that the question of eating Black Pudding is nowhere near as important as questions about personal and sexuality morality. I agreed with her. But then I had to say that God's people in Old Testament times would almost certainly not have agreed with us, nor would the members of the Council in Acts 15 necessarily have agreed. It might be obvious to us, but it would not have been obvious to them. We live in a culture where questions of sexual and personal morality have been much more important that questions about food, though this might be changing now. They lived in a very different culture. My friend was reading the Black Pudding texts through the spectacles of twentieth century British culture and Christian experience and concluding that the Black Pudding issue didn't matter very much and the rule could be ignored. But she objected to what she saw as the Human Sexuality report reading the homosexuality texts through the spectacles of twentieth century British culture and

Christian experience and concluding that the homosexuality issue didn't matter very much and the rule could be ignored. Actually the report says that the issue matters quite a lot, and the texts cannot simply be ignored, but my friend hadn't noticed that.

She had also failed to remember that what's good for the goose is also good for the gander. If she isn't going to take the Black Pudding texts literally, then why should I take too much notice of her if she wants to take the homosexuality ones literally. She is not being consistent. If she examines the Black Pudding texts carefully and seriously and reaches the conclusion that she can eat the stuff, why should she condemn another friend of mine for not taking the Bible seriously when he examines the homosexuality texts carefully and seriously and reaches the conclusion that gay partnerships are okay?

We all examine the Bible every time we read it. We all interpret the Bible. We all read it through our own spectacles. We all decide that this text is more important than that, or that we will accept this teaching but not that. There is no reading without interpreting. Those who oppose the Human Sexuality report can argue that the report interprets the Bible badly, and that it has come to a wrong interpretation of the texts and of the mind of the Bible on this question. They may be right. They may be wrong. But what they cannot do is to say that they take the Bible as it is whereas the report interprets it. That is what my friend was saying, and she cannot have her cake and eat it at the same time, to use another wise old saying. Nor can they say that all of a sudden Methodism has stopped believing the Bible, for the Human Sexuality report uses the same method of interpreting the Bible which Methodism and Methodists have done for years, looking at it as Wesley did with the aid of Tradition, Reason and Experience. You might disagree with the report's conclusions: but you cannot accuse it of not taking the Bible seriously.

So what can we say from the Human Sexuality report about where Methodism stands on the Bible? Opponents of the report say that with this report Methodism has adopted a new and unwelcome stand on the Bible, that

Methodism has shown itself no longer prepared to accept the authority of the Bible. I hope that I have shown that that particular accusation is unfounded. I hope that I have shown that in the report the Methodist Church stands exactly where it does on a number of other questions, adopting a viewpoint contrary to certain Biblical texts or passages, but having come to those conclusions after careful thought about the Bible in the light of Tradition, Reason and Experience. To do this does not deny the central authority of the Bible itself, or if it does then we have denied it many times before.

Nowhere in the report itself, as far as I can see, does anyone grasp the nettle and come out with the statement that, "Although the Bible says No, we will say Yes," though that in effect is more or less what the report ends up by saying. I do not see why we should be afraid to say it. We say it about Black Pudding, divorce and other things. We say it with good reason. This whole book has been written to show why we can say it with a clear conscience.

Saying that the Bible has to be interpreted in each situation, or that we cannot simply read Bible texts straight off but always have to interpret what we read, worries some people. They feel that we are picking and choosing. They worry that if we don't need to believe this bit of the Bible any more, then it won't be long before we've stopped believing any of it. I have tried to show in this book that interpretation is a right and proper thing to do and an essential part of taking the Bible as it is seriously. But folks still worry. They worry about slippery slopes or the thin end of the wedge. It is a real anxiety for some people. We will look at this worry in the next chapter.

13 But what about slippery slopes?

"Slippery slopes" and "thin ends of wedges" are very strong sorts of arguments when people are frightened. And many people today are frightened. Our world is a frightening place. Things are changing so fast, old values are going, places we knew and loved have become dangerous, familiar landmarks are no more. It is no longer safe to go out, or even to stay in. Crime, unemployment, AIDS, poverty, pollution, war, homelessness, terrorism, mass starvation and so many other terrifying things reach right into our living rooms via the telly. Chapels are closing, marriages are breaking down and more and more people don't know where to turn. It's no wonder that people look to the future with dread. Only an ostrich wouldn't.

In this frightening world many people look for reassurance, amid all the uncertainties of daily life they look for certainties, for something to hold on to, something firm and solid. It is natural that Christians should look to their faith to give them this sort of solid certainty. Many Roman Catholics look to the Pope for a clear lead and a definite stand, and in the present hard-line Pope they find it. Many of the growing churches in Britain today are those churches which give their members a clear lead, either through powerful leaders whose instructions the members follow and obey, or through a fundamentalism which says that the Bible has all the answers and all that you need to do is believe it. It is no accident that fundamentalism is growing throughout the modern world and in every world faith, giving us Jewish fundamentalists, Moslem fundamentalists and Hindu fundamentalists as well as Christian ones. And it is the fundamentalists in all faiths who talk most about the dangers of "slippery slopes" and "thin ends of wedges."

Such talk about "slippery slopes" and "thin ends of wedges" is a symptom of the fear and uncertainty of our difficult world. At first it sounds very sensible. If we don't need to believe this part of the Bible any more, then which bits do we need to believe? Before long we won't believe any of it. Then where will we be? But then it starts to falter. If we don't do what the Bible says about gay partnerships it won't be long before we stop doing what it says about adultery, theft and murder will it? Does that really follow? I doubt it. The fear is understandable, but like most fear it starts to disappear as soon as we face up to it.

When we face up to this fear about the Bible it only takes two seconds to recognise that slippery slopes and thin ends of wedges are just red herrings. They do not really exist at all. Christians have always picked and chosen, observed some Bible instructions and decided to take no notice of others. There have always been different interpretations of the Bible, and changes in what is thought to matter and what isn't. There was a huge fuss when some Christians had the nerve to question the teaching of the Bible that slavery was the will of God. Or when others tried to say that the obedience to the king commanded by the Bible was not the last word for the subject. For me personally going against the Bible on divorce, Black Pudding and other things has not stopped me from looking to the Bible for guidance on questions of right and wrong. It has not stopped me from firmly believing that the Bible is to be taken with the utmost seriousness in all our decision-making about faith and morality, or from looking look for a Biblically-based stance on all moral questions.

Using the Bible in the way that all the mainline churches do is not easy, but there is no other way to use it with integrity if we are to take the Bible as it is seriously. Over the centuries Christians have tried to read the Bible seriously, interpret it carefully and prayerfully and come to decisions about what it meant for them there and then. It has never been a simple matter of believing every text or accepting all the Bible's statements as they stand. In this process there have always been slip-ups, some very serious, and there have always been Christians who have gone off the rails. But the Church is still here. So is the Bible.

I can understand why people worry about them: but in this case "slippery slopes" and "thin ends of wedges" are just red herrings.

14 Taking the Bible seriously in other matters too.

So far in this book we have done two things. First we have looked at what the Bible is and how it came to us. We did that because what the Bible is and how it came to us are basic facts which have to be taken into account if we are to debate the authority of the Bible for today's church. Beliefs about the authority and inspiration of the Bible must be solidly founded on the Bible as it is - not simply on what some believers think it is or would like it to be.

Secondly we have looked at the Bible and ethics, at how the Bible can be used in our discussions of Right and Wrong. We did that because there is a serious debate going on in the Methodist Church at the moment about how much notice we should take of certain Bible verses in the complicated question of homosexuality and gay partnerships. We have seen that in many questions of right and wrong the Methodist Church does not simply accept what verses of the Bible say, but looks as well at general principles in the Bible as well as at other factors. Whole books could be written on this subject but I've had to be content with four chapters.

My conviction throughout this book has been that the Bible is essential and vital to Christianity. It is the church's Holy Book, and it must be taken seriously. But to take the Bible seriously begins with understanding and accepting what it is and how it came to us. To read the Bible seriously is to read it as it is. In all its diversity it is the church's special library, its books written and edited by inspired people then selected and agreed by the churches. To take it seriously is to recognise and accept these facts, as well as to look carefully at what it says. This means that on questions of Right and Wrong we look at what the Bible says, and so listen to the received wisdom of our forebears. It does not necessarily mean that we slavishly accept their views. On questions of morality we have seen that the Bible is not a Handbook of Right and Wrong, and that we cannot read it like the Highway Code. To try to do that is not to take the Bible as it is seriously.

In this chapter I want very very briefly to look at what it means to take the Bible as it is seriously in other areas of faith and knowledge. How is the Bible to be read when it talks about things like science, history, the future or the truth? We will glance at each of those four topics in turn.

1 The Bible and Science

When Charles Darwin produced his "<u>Origin of Species</u>" in 1859 there began an uproar in parts of the church which has not died down to this day. Some Christians felt that his findings undermined the authority of the Bible. They believed that the Bible said that God had created the world in six days, and that in those six days he had created all the rich variety of plant and animal species on our planet, and they felt affronted that here was this upstart scientist denying this. If he was right the Bible must be wrong, and that could not be, so science was obviously wrong. And in some quarters science and religion have been at odds ever since. Nowadays there is even a school of thought, slipping into Britain from America, which is trying to insist that the "Bible view that God created the world in six days" is taught in schools as a proper scientific alternative to the Evolutionary view. Such Christians teach that what the Bible says and what science teaches are opposed, and so our young people are forced to choose: the Bible or science?

I am not a scientist, so I cannot comment on the scientific questions. I have not the slightest idea about how the universe began. I do know that at the moment the scientists do not agree on this one, but I also believe that one day, sooner or later, the scientists will work it out and answer the question. I also believe that whatever their answer will be it will be different from what the Bible says, and that does not worry me at all. It does not worry me because the Bible does not give a single and therefore a scientific answer to the question of how the universe came into existence. Those Christians who said to Darwin and who say today that it does and that Genesis 1 is science are guilty of not taking the Bible seriously.

The fact is that there are no less than four different creation "stories" or "pictures" in the Old Testament, each one different from the others. It is wrong to say that it is *the* Bible view that God created the world in six days. What you have to say is that it is *one of* the Bible *views* that he did so. Space prevents me from going into any detail about the four stories but the first is the familiar one in Genesis 1:1-2:4a, where God creates the world in six days and rests on day seven. The second is the story of the garden in Genesis 2:4b-3:24, where things are created in a different order and the climax of the story is about the ambiguity of human life and our spoilt relationships with each other, with nature and with God. Remains of a very ancient creation story can be seen in Psalm 74:12-17, Psalm 89:5-18 and Isaiah 51:9-11 [see also Job 7:12, 26:12, 38:8-11] which talk about creation as God's victory after battle with the monster of chaos. The fourth story or picture is seen in Proverbs 8:22-31 and Job 28:20-28 which uses a different set of pictures about "Wisdom." The great Hymn of Creation in Psalm 104 combines all these four ideas in praise of God the Creator, but no one who reads all these passages and looks at the different pictures used can be left in any doubt that they are just that, four different "pictures" or "stories."

The very fact that we have four different pictures of creation in the Old Testament should warn us against seeing any one of them as a scientific statement about how the world was made. What we have in these stories or pictures is theology and not science, and the stories are profound, fascinating and very relevant as they explore different questions about life and the world from the questions raised by science.

So it is not that Darwin's theory of evolution contradicts Genesis 1, it is that Genesis 2 contradicts Genesis 1. Both cannot be scientifically accurate, while the third and fourth pictures don't look remotely "scientific" anyway. To read the Bible as a science book not only asks the Bible the wrong sort of questions, but it also fails to take the Bible as it is seriously.

2 The Bible and History

If Genesis 1 and Genesis 2 are not science and are not a factual statement of what actually happened at the beginning of the world and the beginning of history, what about the chapters that follow? What about Cain and Abel, Noah and the Flood, Abraham and Sarah, Sodom and Gomorrah, Jacob and Esau, Joseph in Egypt, Moses and the Exodus, Joshua and the battle of Jericho, David and Solomon and so on right on down to Daniel in the Lion's Den and to Jesus of Nazareth?

Let us start at the end. In chapter 7 we looked at how the stories about Jesus came to be written in the four gospels that we have. When it comes to Jesus of Nazareth there are certain facts that we can be sure of and they are these: that he was a charismatic Galilean prophet with recognised gifts of healing, who taught using parables and gathered disciples around him, and who died by crucifixion in Jerusalem "under Pontius Pilate." Those are the facts of his life, recognised by historians Christian, Jewish and secular: but Christians want to say more than that, and the four Gospels do say more. The gospel writers are followers of Jesus, and we saw in John 20:31 that John wrote his gospel

> *"so that you may come to believe that Jesus is the Messiah, the Son of God, and that through believing you may have life in his name."*

In his gospel, his *message of good news*, John gives us facts of Jesus's life plus an interpretation of what it all means, and it is not always clear which is which. That is what all history is: fact plus interpretation. We saw in chapter 5 that the New Testament is not interested in accuracy of detail, like who exactly discovered the Empty Tomb, nor in precise dates, like when such an important event as the cleansing of the Temple occured. As such the New Testament is a poor history textbook. What the New Testament is really interested in is showing that Jesus of Nazareth is the clue to the meaning of life, the universe and God. It is a theology book rather than a history book.

The same can be said about the "history books" of the Old Testament [Joshua, Judges, Samuel, Kings and

Chronicles]. We saw that they too are not always reliable history. It is not really accurate to call them "History Books" at all, for the Hebrew Bible calls Joshua to 2 Kings the "Former Prophets" showing that they are really theology books. They are about God, his will and his ways. At the same time most Old Testament history scholars would say that we are still on the bedrock of fact, in general if not in detail, as far back as Moses and Exodus. A few would even say that we are on the bedrock of fact as far back as Abraham. But that is as far as it goes, if it does go that far. Beyond that we have stories with no factual or historical basis. But that does not mean that the stories in Genesis have no value. Their teaching about God, and about the meaning of life, the universe and everything is far more profound than we Christians sometimes give the Old Testament credit for. That is why they were told, preserved and valued.

A story does not need to be historically or factually true to be good theology. Think of the story of the Good Samaritan, the story of the prophet Jonah, or the story of Ruth and Naomi. We would think that an archaeologist who went to Israel to look for the inn on the Jericho road had missed the point somewhere. So have those who argue about whales swallowing people.

3 The Bible and the Future

The writers of the New Testament have an interesting way of reading the older scriptures. They don't seem to care at all about what the original writers might have meant, and they lift all kinds of sayings out of their original contexts to illustrate what they believe about Jesus. I think their reasoning was that as the older scriptures were about God, and as Jesus was God with us, so everything in the older scriptures could teach us about Jesus. Be that as it may we can see Matthew doing this very clearly in the first two chapters of his gospel where he uses five quotes from the older scriptures to illustrate things about the birth of Jesus. Only the second talks about the coming of the Messiah at all, and we can't even find the last one in the Old Testament. But Matthew believed that the old scriptures pointed forward to Jesus, and in particular that the prophets predicted the coming of the Messiah.

Some of them did, but there was more to prophecy than predicting the future. Some prophecy was more like what we would call counselling, and much prophecy was what we would call preaching: but there was also warning about the future and some prediction. What the New Testament does is to lead to us to think that all prophecy is prediction, and all prophecy is about the future. This distorts our understanding of the Old Testament, but it also makes us go wrong when we think of the Bible and the future.

The New Testament ends on what seems to be a look into the future and a prediction about the End of the World. And in these frightening times some find the Book of Revelation to be an exciting and reassuring book, for when things like the end of the Russian Communist Empire or the Gulf War happen they can see this as the fulfillment of a verse here or there in Revelation [or in Daniel or Ezekiel 38-39]. The end is near, wars and famines testify to it, so we can hold on in faith for our deliverence is at hand. Others try to read Revelation or other parts of the Bible like it, and give up: monsters, numbers, visions, angels, secret signs and weird imagery is too much for them. Both groups fail to take the Bible seriously here, for this special kind of literature has a real place and purpose: but it is not to predict the future. It is to assure struggling believers that God is indeed the King of the Universe; to give them that assurance now when the forces of evil seem so strong, and to reassure them that in the end, as we say in the Lord's Prayer, his kingdom will come and his will will be done. The strange ideas and pictures make sense when you know the conventions of the literature you are reading. When you are taking Tolkien's <u>Lord of the Rings</u> seriously you don't ask where "Middle Earth" is, or about the biology of orcs or hobbits.

<u>4   The Bible and truth</u>

Most Methodists don't say the great Creeds of the Christian Faith very often, but they are there in the <u>Methodist Service Book</u> and we all say them occasionally. Other Christians say them much more often. These Creeds are lists of what the Church believes, and if someone were to ask us what we believe our natural way of answering them would probably be to give them a list of the things we believe. It might be a long list or it might be a short one; it might include parts of the great Christian Creeds or it might not. But we would make a list. Likewise if someone asked what the Liberal Party believed, or what Friends of the Earth believed, their spokespersons would in all probability reply by giving a list. For us it is natural to make a list of the things we believe: but it is not so with the Bible.

There is nothing like a Creed in the Bible, neither in the Old Testament nor the New. The nearest that the Old Testament possesses is the "Shema," the four mysterious words, impossible to translate precisely as the different versions in the margin show, of Deuteronomy 6:4,

"Hear, O Israel: The LORD is our God, the LORD alone."

The nearest we come to a creed in the New Testament is the confession of faith that we find several times which says, *"Jesus is Lord."*

But nowhere in the Bible do we find a list of things to believe about God such as we have in the Christian Creeds. The Bible does not do it that way. Instead the Bible tells stories, all sorts of stories, just as Jesus used parables, stories about God and his people. There are never any definitions of God or truth, and there are not always any explanations of what the stories mean. Jesus often ended his parables by saying,

"If you have ears to hear, then hear!"

and it is as if we have to read the Bible with those words ringing in our ears.

In this chapter I have talked about the Bible doing its theology by telling stories, and I have mentioned creation "stories" or "pictures" and the "stories" of Abraham, Moses, Jonah and Jesus. For me the old Sunday School hymn gets it exactly right when it says,

"God has given us a book full of stories."

But John Betjeman's poem, "Christmas," has a haunting

phrase that repeats three times, "And is it true?"
After five verses about Christmassy things we read,

> "And is it true? And is it true,
> This most tremendous tale of all,
> Seen in a stained-glass window"s hue,
> A Baby in an ox's stall?
> The Maker of the stars and sea
> Become a Child on earth for me?

And is it true?..." That is the question that people keep on asking about these stories. Betjeman calls the Christmas scene a "tale." I have talked about the Bible and its "stories." Are they "true" stories? is the inevitable, though I believe wrong, question that people keep asking. And the answer of course is that it all depends on what you mean by "true." Some of the stories are true to history, in outline if not in detail. Many are true to life, too true to life to be comfortable some of them. Some are true in the sense that prose is true, others in the sense that poetry or parables are true. Not all, perhaps not most of the Old Testament ones at least, are "factually" true. But all of them were told by their tellers in the conviction that they were true to the way things really were, to God, his will and his ways. When we read the stories, no less than when we try to see what the Bible says about right and wrong, we read them to see what they have to say to us today. And we need to read them in the light of that same mobile, trying to make sense of them through what the Church has made of them over the years and asking how they relate to our experience of God and his world. The best question to ask the Bible is not, Did this happen? or, Is this true? but, What does this say to us about God, about life, about faith?

This chapter has been about taking the Bible as it is seriously. To take the Bible seriously means that we must not treat it as a Handbook of Right and Wrong or a textbook of Science or History, nor like an Old Moore's Alamanac about the future, or even an Encyclopaedia of Theology where we look up the answers to our questions. It is a book of many parts, as we have seen. Much of it is a book of stories which our faithful forebears told because they spoke to them of God, and which those who heard treasured and valued and passed on down to us.

15   But what about the nasty bits?

Before we come to the last chapter this is another little interlude to comment on a problem which perplexes some sensitive readers of the Bible - what about the nasty bits?

Among the nasty bits in the Bible are obviously the gory bits. There are plenty of these, and not only in the Old Testament either. These are the bits that the children seem to enjoy best. Why is it that the most thumbed pages of illustrated Childrens' Bibles are Sodom and Gommorah getting destroyed by a thunderbolt, the Egyptian soldiers drowning in the Red Sea or King Herod staring at John the Baptist's head on a platter? Life in those days was often nasty, brutish and short and the old stories of the Bible reflect that quite accurately. Which is what you would expect if the writers of the Bible were real people.

But there are worse parts of the Bible than the gory bits. There are the really nasty bits - the bits where the Bible applauds horrible things and approves of things that everyone these days knows to be quite wrong or primitive or barbaric. I am only going to give one example of these and it is from the New Testament. I could have picked some choice ones from the Old Testament, like the last two verses of Psalm 137, but the one I have picked comes from one of Paul's letters in the New Testament. Other examples from the New Testament might be the way that it applauds God's capital punishment of Ananias and Sapphira for telling fibs to the Church Council [Acts 5:1-11], or where it approves of slavery [Ephesians 6:5, Colossians 3:22 and Titus 2:9], or even where it insists that wives must be subservient to their husbands [Ephesians 5:22-24, 1 Peter 3:1].

My example is Paul's outburst against Christians who thought differently than he did on the question of whether or not gentile men who became Christians should be circumcised. He wrote,

> "I wish those who unsettle you would castrate themselves!"
>
> [Galatians 5:12]

Here is a simple example of a Christian leader who has lost his temper, and whose secretary does not have the sense to miss that outburst out of the dictation he is taking. Here Paul is extremely angry at people who hold a different view on an issue which he regards as central to the Christian Faith. And it was a central issue. If Paul's opponents had won that debate our Christianity today would be a very different thing than it is, if it existed at all. Here in this verse is someone a long way from loving his enemies and praying for those who were persecuting him. Here is someone whose outburst we can understand and sympathise with - at least I can. But here too is a verse of the Bible, out of a letter in which Paul gives advice and instruction to the Christians in Galatia.

What are we to do with this nasty bit? Are we to say that this outburst shows that in the Letter to the Galatians all that we have is an all too human Paul giving his opinions to the Galatians, and that if he has thoughts as bad as that it is obvious that we need not take that or anything else he writes as gospel truth? You could think that: but if you do out goes the baby with the bathwater. Or are we to say that because this verse is in the Bible, then obviously Paul must be right in what he thinks of his enemies, and God would be happy for Paul to get rid of them in whatever way he could? You could think that: but you then end up saying that it is okay to be abusive, and how does that square with loving your enemy?

The nasty bits in the Bible are there. The people who wrote them might not have thought they were nasty at all: but we do, or some people do. Most twentieth century Christians believe that gratuitous violence is wrong, but it looks as if some of the writers of the Old Testament enjoyed it. Most twentieth century Christians I know do not believe that wives should be subservient to husbands, but several New Testament writers did. I call those bits "nasty bits" but the writers would not have seen them that way. Nowadays we would be rightly considered to be nasty if we held those sort of views or behaved in that sort of way. These nasty bits show that the writers were very much the people of their time, who else could they be? They also show us how times have changed. They show the "human element" in the Bible, God's message earthed in a particular time and place and person. We do not need to throw the Bible out just because we don't like the nasty bits. We don't have to say that the nasty bits aren't nasty just because they are in the Bible either.

Knowing what the Bible is and how it got to us explains how the nasty bits are there. That and our "mobile theology" explains how we can deal with them.

16 The last word?

Let me begin this last chapter with a favourite quotation, which among other things makes the point that there will never be a *last word* about the Bible. It is supposed to have been said by the Pilgrim Father, John Robinson, who left Plymouth on the Mayflower in 1620. It is a famous one and for me it sums up why we must read and also study and interpret the Bible,

"The Lord has yet more light and truth to bring forth from his Word."

The quote calls the Bible God's "Word," and I have tried to show in this book how God speaks to us in and through the Bible. He did not dictate it word by word. God's Word as we have it in the Bible has come through the minds, lips and pens of priests and prophets, saints and theologians of old, checked, filtered and edited by the church over centuries until the Bibles we have today were agreed by the fourth century AD. How then should we think of the Bible? In the book I have quoted two hymns, the old one by the Bishop,

"O Word of God incarnate,
O wisdom from on high,
O truth unchanged, unchanging,
O light of our dark sky...."

and the new one by Brian Wren,

".... some, remembering the past,
Recorded what they knew,
And some, in letters or laments,
In prophecy and praise,
Recovered, held and re-expressed
New hope for changing days.

For all the writings that survived,
For leaders long ago,
Who sifted, chose, and then preserved

> *The Bible that we know,*
> *Give thanks...."*

[Hymns and Psalms 447, "Deep in the shadows of the past" by Brian A Wren (1936 -). Reprinted by permission of Oxford University Press]

It is hard to be sure who the Bishop is praising in this verse of his hymn. A friend tried to convince me once that the Bishop is praising our Lord Jesus Christ, who is the "Word of God incarnate", and who is our Wisdom, Truth and Light. But I am not convinced. Whatever the Bishop meant I am sure that many who sing this hymn are praising the Bible as they sing these words, and that seems to me to be the natural way to understand this verse in the light of the three verses that follow it in our hymn book. If that is so then the Bishop has surely got it seriously wrong, unless he is using gorgeous poetry which is not to be taken literally. Whichever it is he has left us a dangerous hymn, because it encourages us to worship the Bible itself. By contrast Brian Wren's hymn is mundane and down to earth, and much more accurate because it reflects the Bible as it is and how it has come to us.

From the earliest chapters of the Old Testament we read warnings against worshipping and putting our faith and trust in anything other than God himself. So I get worried when I sometimes hear Christians saying that we should *believe in* the Bible. I do not *believe in* the Bible. I *believe in* Jesus Christ: he is the only one in whom I put my faith and trust, and through whom I worship God the Father. It is only a short step from saying that we *believe in* the Bible, to putting our trust and faith in the Bible, and so to worshipping it as an idol, which the Bishop's hymn comes very near to doing. That is bad in itself, but also if we treat the Bible as an idol what do we do about the feet of clay?

It is not easy to read, study and interpret the Bible. To do it we have to bring "*all our heart, and soul, and mind, and strength*" to the task. This is what I have been trying to do in this book. Some of the conclusions reached from studying the Bible as it is may be at odds with what some Christians think or have thought about the Bible. I do not apologise for that.

My conclusions have not been reached because I do not believe the Bible or take it seriously - the very opposite is the case. They have been reached by taking the Bible as it is very seriously and by reading what it says very carefully. You cannot accuse modern scholarship of failing to take the Bible seriously, and I hope you won't accuse me of it either.

So finally to the Bible and deciding about right and wrong. I can do no better than use a phrase from another hymn. Given the Bible as it is, it looks as if the Bible must be *"our guide, and not our chain."* Nowhere in the Human Sexuality report does anyone grasp the nettle and come out with the statement that, "In this case although the Bible says No, we will say Yes," although that in fact is more or less what the report ends up by saying. I do not see why we should be afraid to say this sort of thing. Whether we should say it in the matters discussed in that report is not the point of this book. The point of this book is that it is a question open for discussion. We say it about Black Pudding, and about divorce and other major things. We say it with good reason. This book has shown why we can say it with a clear conscience and still call ourselves "Bible Christians."

17 Some books and things about the Bible.

First the "things:"

1 I quoted from the <u>Faith and Worship</u> training course for Local Preachers once or twice in the book. Most of the Circuits in the Cornwall District are running this course, and there is no reason why non-preachers should not join in the groups, or experienced preachers either come to that. Or ask your minister to set up a study group to look at one or two of the units [the Introduction to the Bible one is Unit 5].

2 Most areas of the country are covered by courses arranged by the Education Officer of the local Anglican Diocese, and in Cornwall we have an ecumenical network called the <u>Cornish Churches' Courses and Workshops.</u> Courses on the Old and New Testaments are laid on regularly, as well as many other courses. Ask your minister for a leaflet.

3 There are also all kinds of courses run by University extra-mural departments all over the place.

Second - books. This is much more difficult because there are hundreds at all levels. What follows is a basic list of introductory books, all under a fiver:

1 <u>The Bible From Scratch</u> by Simon Jenkins and published by Lion is a superb "cartoon-style" guide to all the books of the Bible from Genesis to Revelation. Lion also produce a <u>User's Guide to the Bible</u> by C Wright.

2 The Methodist Publishing House publish an <u>ABC of the Bible</u> in two parts by J M Furness, a little pamphlet <u>How can I believe the Bible?</u> by D Hatton, a look at some Old Testament stories <u>Look at Them This Way</u> by N Price, and <u>The Light of the Living</u> by D E R Isett.

3 <u>What is the Bible?</u> by J Barton, published by SPCK, is "the ideal book for anyone seeking some sound advice on how to read the Bible intelligently." SPCK also publish a <u>Pocket Guide to the Bible</u> by J O Gooch and J A Keller.

4 A very good series of Bible Study Notes is the <u>Guidelines</u> series by the Bible Reading Fellowship.